ABOUT CANADA

HEALTH
AND ILLNESS

ABOUT CANADA

HEALTH
AND ILLNESS

Second Edition

DENNIS RAPHAEL

FERNWOOD
PUBLISHING

HALIFAX & WINNIPEG

Editing: Brenda Conroy
Design: John van der Woude
Printed and bound in Canada by Hignell Book Printing

Published in Canada by Fernwood Publishing
32 Oceanvista Lane, Black Point, Nova Scotia, B0J 1B0
and 748 Broadway Avenue, Winnipeg, MB R3G 0X3
www.fernwoodpublishing.ca

Fernwood Publishing Company Limited gratefully acknowledges the financial support of the Government of Canada through the Canada Book Fund and the Canada Council for the Arts, the Nova Scotia Department of Communities, Culture and Heritage, the Manitoba Department of Culture, Heritage and Tourism under the Manitoba Publishers Marketing Assistance Program and the Province of Manitoba, through the Book Publishing Tax Credit, for our publishing program.

   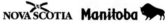

Library and Archives Canada Cataloguing in Publication

Raphael, Dennis, author
Health and illness / Dennis Raphael. -- 2nd edition.

(About Canada series ; 4)
Includes bibliographical references and index.
Issued in print and electronic formats.
ISBN 978-1-55266-826-9 (paperback).--ISBN 978-1-55266-902-0 (epub).--
ISBN 978-1-55266-903-7 (kindle)

1. Public health--Social aspects--Canada. 2. Public health--Economic aspects--Canada. 3. Medical policy--Social aspects--Canada. 4. Social medicine--Canada. I. Title. II. Series: About Canada series ; 4

RA449.R36 2016   362.10971   C2016-904980-9
C2016-904981-7

CONTENTS

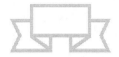

ACKNOWLEDGEMENTS

One of the greatest pleasures of my professional life has been the opportunity to meet and work with committed researchers and policy advocates from across Canada — people from the wide range of sectors that have come to be known as representing the social determinants of health. Much of this book represents an integration and synthesis of their work, and I have made every attempt to recognize and communicate their contributions.

These individuals include Carolyne Alix, Laura Anderson, Pat Armstrong, Nathalie Auger, Toba Bryant, Tracey Burns, Ann Curry-Stevens, Janice Foley, Martha Friendly, Grace-Edward Galabuzi, Lars Hallstrom, Michelle Firestone, Andrew Jackson, Ronald Labonte, David Langille, Elizabeth McGibbon, Lynn McIntyre, Barbara Ronson McNichol, Michael Polanyi, Govind Rao, Irving Rootman, Michael Shapcott, Peter Smith, Janet Smylie, Emile Tompa, Diane-Gabrielle Tremblay, Valerie Tarasuk and Charles Ungerleider.

All of these people practise what University of Washington professor Katharyne Mitchell calls "public scholarship." They recognize the need to move their research findings and recommendations beyond the academy in the service of influencing public policy. Their activities have promoted better understandings of what needs to be done.

But to date our attempts to prod our governments and elected representatives to implement health-promoting public policy have fallen well short of what is being accomplished in other nations. This book is one more attempt to move this agenda forward.

I am very appreciative of Fernwood Publishing — especially Wayne Antony and Beverley Rach — and the others involved in producing this book — Brenda Conroy and Debbie Mathers — for their support of this effort.

In these difficult times, it will do us well to recall Bertolt Brecht's words from his poem "The World's One Hope."

> All those who have thought about the bad state of things
> refuse to appeal to the compassion of one group of people
> for another.
> But the compassion of the oppressed for the oppressed
> is indispensable.
> It is the world's one hope.

WHO STAYS HEALTHY?
WHO GETS SICK?

The high burden of illness responsible for appalling premature loss of life arises in large part because of the conditions in which people are born, grow, live, work, and age — conditions that together provide the freedom people need to live lives they value. — World Health Organization[1]

"It's not as if we won't die. We all die," Nancy Krieger of Harvard University's School of Public Health reminds us. "The question is: At what age? With what degree of suffering? With what degree of preventable illness?"[2]

Staying healthy and avoiding disease and early death is probably one of the greatest concerns of all Canadians. But how do we go about doing this? What do we know about keeping Canadians alive and healthy for as long as possible?

In the traditional model of health, the body is seen as a machine that is either running well or in need of repair. If it is infected with germs or afflicted with system or organ malfunctioning, the remedy lies in medical or curative care, which is located in the health care system and administered by doctors and nurses. Canadians are therefore urged to pay attention to medical discoveries and treatment — especially access to doctors and hospitals — and to be mindful of how our "lifestyle choices" could affect these problems. Newspapers, television, documentaries and other media overflow with information about hospital costs, wait times, the supply of doctors, and what to eat and why we should exercise. While any individual experiencing illness will certainly value medical treatment, this traditional model of health says little if anything about what drives most diseases and illnesses.

Decades of research and hundreds of studies in Canada tell the real story about the important factors that make us healthy or ill. The factors that give us longer, healthy lives or shorter, sick lives are not these much-discussed medical and lifestyle ingredients, but rather the living and working conditions we experience from day to day. The World Health Organization calls these health-shaping characteristics the "social determinants of health" (SDoH). This term has become widely used and accepted in the last couple of decades.[3] In a nutshell, SDoH refers to the social and economic conditions that shape whether people and groups of people are healthy or ill. The Health Council of Canada recognizes the importance of the SDoH and provides a description of these social determinants:

> The reality is that our health — and our ability to live a healthy lifestyle — is affected by a … [broad] range of factors. These factors, called the [social] determinants of health, include how much money we have, our early childhood experiences, and our level of education. They include whether or not we work (and the kind of work we do), our relationships with family and friends, how connected we are to our communities and society, whether we have easy access to affordable healthy food, and the quality of our

health care services. Belonging to a specific racial, ethnic, or cultural group can also influence our health.[4]

It would be comforting to believe we can choose these living and working conditions, but in most cases they are imposed upon us as a result of our position in society — our social class, gender, race and other aspects of our personal circumstances. The quality of these health-shaping living and working conditions is strongly affected by how our capitalist market economy creates and distributes income and wealth. In a market economy, the great majority of individuals participate in paid employment in order to survive. What this paid employment looks like and the wages it provides are largely determined by the corporations and businesses that hire people. This is less the case in many wealthy, developed nations, which unlike Canada, make greater efforts to regulate the workplace and make sure people have economic security if they are unable to work or find work.[5]

In Canada, our elected representatives and policy-makers make decisions that shape these living and working conditions that determine whether we are healthy or ill. These public policies can provide — or not provide — job training, living wages, universal child-care, affordable housing and social services that improve or worsen these health-influencing living and working conditions. Public policies are the collective outcome of the decisions made by people elected to federal, provincial and municipal legislatures and the government advisors and civil servants who counsel these elected members of governments. Governments at all levels enact policies, laws and regulations that influence how much income Canadians receive through employment, social assistance, pensions and levels of taxation. Policies, laws and regulations also shape the quality and availability of affordable housing, health care, social services and recreational opportunities, and even what happens when Canadians lose their jobs during economic downturns, such as the one that Canada began experiencing in 2008 and many believe is continuing to this day.[6]

Our elected representatives also determine whether or not children have access to affordable and quality child-care and good schools, whether or not parents experience good working conditions, and whether seniors receive public pensions that allow them to live in dignity. We have always known that these areas of public policy-making influence our general quality of life, but we now recognize that they also shape our health, since these policies determine both the quality and the distribution among Canadians of the social determinants of health.

The interaction of government public policy with how the economic system operates determines in large part the social

The 1 percent influence health and illness
The corporate sector has organized to increase corporate profits by:

- supporting high-level agreements that facilitate world trade and investment at the expense of secure and well-paying jobs for most Canadians; and
- urging governments to reduce taxes on corporations and the wealthy, which reduces governments' ability to provide economic and social security for most Canadians. Governments now offer fewer programs and services to their citizens, which has led to a serious erosion of the living and working conditions that promote health and prevent illness.

Source: David Langille, 2016, "Follow the Money: How Business and Politics Define our Health," in D. Raphael (ed.), Social Determinants of Health: Canadian Perspectives, third edition, Canadian Scholars' Press.

determinants of health we experience, and this interaction is frequently a site of conflict. In Canada, members of the corporate and business sector are the strongest voices against regulating our market economy. They call for public policies that favour owners and managers of business at the expense of workers. They lobby governments to weaken employment regulations, thereby lowering wages and providing fewer benefits. They also call for the health care and social programs that benefit most Canadians to be reduced. The ongoing conflict between the interests of the business and corporate sector and the interests of most Canadians is an important part of the SDoH story in Canada.

The social determinants of health are crucial for the health of Canadians. If we can understand what they are, how they are distributed and how they get "under our skin" to cause either health or illness, we can act to improve them, which will allow us to live longer and healthier lives.

HISTORICAL PERSPECTIVES
ON HEALTH AND ILLNESS

A concern with the social determinants of health is nothing new. In the fourth century BCE, the Greek philosopher Plato considered how living conditions — particularly inequality — affected society. In *The Laws*, he commented:

> In a state which is desirous of being saved from the greatest of all plagues — not faction [conflict], but rather distraction [failure to reach our highest potential]; there should exist among the citizens neither extreme poverty, nor, again, excess of wealth, for both are productive of both these evils.

During the mid-nineteenth century, German political economist Friedrich Engels showed how the living situations of working-class people in England caused the infections and diseases that killed at an early age. In *The Condition of the Working Class in England,* Engels gave the same reasons for ill health accepted by modern-day health researchers. He stated that unhealthy living conditions (e.g., poor working conditions, housing and food), day-to-day stress (e.g., uncertainty and hopelessness) and the adoption of health-threatening coping behaviours (e.g., alcohol consumption and sexual indulgence) caused disease and early death.

At the same time, German medical doctor Rudolph Virchow argued that living conditions that caused disease and death were rooted in public policy-making. He identified how politics — decisions about *who gets what, when and how* — could either promote or prevent disease. His 1845 *Report on the Typhus Epidemic in Upper*

Condition of the working class in England in 1845

"All conceivable evils are heaped upon the poor....

They are given damp dwellings, cellar dens that are not waterproof from below or garrets that leak from above.... They are supplied bad, tattered, or rotten clothing, adulterated and indigestible food. They are exposed to the most exciting changes of mental condition, the most violent vibrations between hope and fear.... They are deprived of all enjoyments except sexual indulgence and drunkenness and are worked every day to the point of complete exhaustion of their mental and physical energies."

Source: Friedrich Engels, 1987/1845), The Condition of the Working Class in England, Penguin Classics, p. 129.

Silesia — a Polish province of Prussia — concluded that lack of democracy, feudal practices and unfair tax policies created the poor living conditions, inadequate diet and problems of hygiene that fuelled the typhus epidemic. Since then, concern with societal conditions and how they shape health and cause illness has ebbed and flowed. Focus has been diverted to medical treatments of bodies and their organs (biomedical approach) and reducing behavioural risk factors (healthy lifestyles approach) rather than public policy decisions that shape the distribution of resources.[7]

Interest in the societal causes of health and illness was reignited by publication in the United Kingdom of the 1980 *Black Report* and the 1987 *The Health Divide.* These reports described how — despite universal access to health care — Britons in unskilled manual jobs were more likely to develop and die early from a number of diseases

Diseases are the result of defects of society

German physician Rudolph Virchow's (1821–1902) medical discoveries are so extensive that he is known as the "father of modern pathology." But he was also a trailblazer in identifying how societal policies shape health. Virchow stated: "Disease is not something personal and special, but only a manifestation of life under modified (pathological) conditions.... Medicine is a social science and politics is nothing else but medicine on a large scale.... If medicine is to fulfil her great task, then she must enter the political and social life. Do we not always find the diseases of the populace traceable to defects in society?"

Source: Rudolph Virchow, 1985/1848, Collected Essays on Public Health and Epidemiology, *Science History Publications.*

and injuries at every stage of the life. The differences occurred in a step-by-step progression. Professionals and their children had the best health (living longer with less illness), followed by white-collar skilled workers and blue collar skilled workers, with manual labourers experiencing the worst health (living short and more sick lives). These reports concluded that inequalities in health were primarily due to differences in living and working conditions and not to differences in health attitudes or behaviours. In 1998 and 2010, two more U.K. government inquiries came to similar conclusions about the importance of living and working conditions as the primary determinants of health.[8]

CANADIAN PERSPECTIVES

Canada also made important contributions to understanding how living and working conditions and public policies determine health. In 1974 a federal government report, *A New Perspective on the Health of Canadians,* was one of the first modern statements on the role that the environment — broadly defined — played in shaping health. Another Canadian government document, *Achieving Health for All: A Framework for Health Promotion,* argued in 1986 that health could be improved by public policies that provided Canadians with secure living conditions.[9]

The Canadian Public Health Association (CPHA) has been saying the same thing for over three decades. Its 1996 *Action Statement for Health Promotion in Canada* advocated for new public policies as the single best way to improve the health of Canadians. The CPHA said that the government should reduce the income gap between the rich and poor and help communities overcome bad living conditions. In 2000, the association recognized poverty as a severe threat to health and called for its reduction. These and other CPHA reports drew attention to the harmful health effects of unemployment, income insecurity, homelessness and economic insecurity. For its part, the Canadian Senate produced five reports emphasizing the importance of the SDoH and of working to improve living and working conditions.[10]

The World Health Organization's Commission on Social Determinants of Health was a major undertaking that had significant Canadian involvement. The Canadian government provided funding to the Commission, and Monique Bégin, the former federal minister of health and welfare, served as a commissioner. Canadian researchers headed up the *Early Child Development* and *Globalization and Health* knowledge networks. The final report of the Commission and the reports of its various knowledge hubs provide extensive evidence of the importance of living and working conditions and recommendations for public policy action.[11]

HOW IMPORTANT ARE THE SOCIAL DETERMINANTS OF HEALTH?

The health of Canadians is not distributed equally — some people die younger and some people are sicker than others. This inequality is a result of the quality and distribution of the social determinants of health. The SDoH are not distributed in a fair and just manner — i.e., rich people have too much income and poor people not enough — and *unfair* and *unjust* differences in health result from this —i.e., rich people live much longer and are much healthier than poor people.

Health inequities — unfair differences in health outcomes among Canadians of differing income, gender, race or other social characteristics — are demonstrable and measurable. There are two ways to measure health inequities. The first method focuses on death rates (called mortality) among groups. These indicators include how long

Health inequality and health inequity

"Health inequality is the generic term used to designate differences, variations, and disparities in the health achievements and risk factors of individuals and groups .... [It is] a descriptive term that need not imply moral judgment."

"*Health inequity* refers to those inequalities in health that are deemed to be unfair or stemming from some form of injustice.... On one account, most of the health inequalities across social groups (such as class and race) are unjust because they reflect an unfair distribution of the underlying social determinants of health (for example, access to educational opportunities, safe jobs, health care and the social bases of self respect)."

Source: I. Kawachi, S.V. Subramanian and N. Almeida-Filho, 2002, "A Glossary for Health Inequalities," Journal of Epidemiology and Community Health *56 (9), pp. 647–48.*

people live (life expectancy), how early they die (premature years of life lost to a specific age, say seventy-five years), whether infants die within one year of being born (infant mortality rates) and death from various diseases or injuries (disease-specific mortality rates). The second approach focuses on the presence of disease and injuries (called morbidity) and includes measures of babies being born small (low birth-weight rates), the number of new cases of a disease or injuries (incidence) and the number of people with a disease at a point in time (prevalence). Measures of morbidity also include subjective self-reports of health (e.g., a person's estimations of whether their health is excellent, good, fair or poor) or objective measures, such as a diagnosis of an illness or problem (e.g., diagnosis of heart disease or lack of mobility).

The richest Canadians outlive the poorest

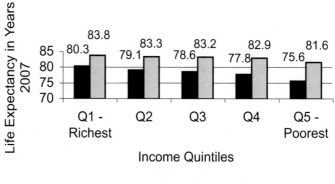

Data Sources: Statistics Canada, Canadian Vital Statistics, Birth and Death Databases and population estimates; Canadian Community Health Survey; National Population Health Survey, Health institutions component; Residential Care Facilities Survey; Canadian Health Measures Survey; Census of population.

Inequities in Life Expectancy and Death

Not surprisingly, Canadians do not all live to the same age. Even though our average life expectancy is about eighty-one years, considerable variation exists. For example, in 2007, differences in life expectancy were almost five years between the lowest and highest income Canadian men and differences were over two years for Canadian women. These differences among Canadian income groups are graded from wealthiest to poorest, a phenomenon called the "social gradient" in health.[12]

Inequities in Sickness and Injuries

Birth weight is also a function of income. A low birth-weight rate is an important indicator of health because it is associated with a wide range of health problems across the lifespan. In Canada, low

Poorer kids are hospitalized more often for injuries than wealthier kids

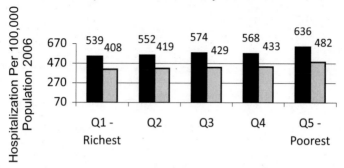

Neighbourhood Income Quintile

■ Males ☐ Females

Sources: National Trauma Registry Minimum Data Set Canadian Institute for Health Information;
Fichier des hospitalisations med-écho, ministère de la Santé et des Services sociaux du Québec; 2006
Census, Statistics Canada.

birth-weight rates are 7.1/100 in the wealthiest areas and 9.9/100 in the poorest areas, a difference of 39 percent.[13]

The same patterns hold for childhood injury. Across Canada in 2008–09, girls and boys living in the poorest neighbourhoods had hospitalization injury rates that were 18 percent higher than girls and boys living in the wealthiest neighbourhoods.[14]

GENETICS, RISK FACTORS AND RISK CONDITIONS

Given that diseases result from problems with the workings of our bodies, many people see unlocking the human genome as the key to ending illness as we know it, but there is little evidence to support this idea. Very few diseases are caused by the operation of a single or even multiple genes, and even when such genes are found they usually provide only a small clue as to whether an individual will get a disease. Discoveries related to the human genome certainly will not influence the health of Canadians in general, especially in regards to the main killers — cancers and heart and respiratory diseases, as these are related to the effects of environment rather than the simple unfolding of genetic dispositions.[15]

A similar situation exists in regard to risk factors, or what has come to be known as "healthy lifestyle choices." Canadians have become well aware of the "holy trinity of risk": unhealthy diet, lack of physical activity and tobacco use. Indeed, Canadians have overwhelmingly internalized these messages. Disturbingly, studies find that Canadians have little appreciation of how their health is profoundly shaped by living and working conditions, that is, the SDoH.[16] This may be changing.

All things being equal, it is probably better for us to eat a nutritious diet, be physically active and avoid tobacco and excessive alcohol use. But the narrow focus on "risk factors" has led to a profound neglect by governments, policy-makers, public health agencies, the media and disease associations of how societal "risk conditions" are far more important influences upon health. It does not help that Canadians' lack of awareness of the importance of the social determinants of health provides no incentives for authorities to shift their approach to promoting the health of Canadians despite the evidence.

A major study in Ontario illustrates the relative importance of "risk conditions" versus "risk factors." People were asked to describe their health as being excellent, very good, good, fair or poor, and they also provided objective evidence of their health status (for example, vision, hearing, mobility, pain, etc.), which created a "functional health" score for each of them. These self-reported health scores and functional health scores were related to a number of risk conditions and risk factors.

Compared to those under 40, those aged 40–64 years had a 77 percent greater likelihood of having low functional health scores and more than twice the risk of the youngest group for reporting "fair" or "poor health." For the 65-plus age group, the corresponding risks of these adverse health outcomes were almost three times greater for poor functional and for reporting poor or fair health. Clearly, aging is an important aspect of health.

Low income, however, is associated with an almost four times greater risk of reporting poor or fair health and a two and a half times greater risk of having lower functional health than high-income. Being of middle income also increases reporting poor or fair health by 62 percent and the risk of lower functional health by 34 percent, as compared to high-income earners. Smoking and doing no exercise did increase health risk, but by much lower amounts than did the risk condition of being middle or low income.[17]

Another study provided similar findings. Statistics Canada examined the predictors of life expectancy, disability-free life expectancy and the presence of fair or poor health among residents of 136 regions across Canada. The predictors included socio-demographic factors, or risk conditions (the proportions of Aboriginal and visible minority populations, unemployment rate, population size, percentage of population aged 65 or over, average income and average number of years of schooling). Also considered were the risk factors of smoking rates, obesity, infrequent exercise, heavy drinking, high stress and depression.[18]

Once again risk factors (behaviours) were shown to be weak predictors of health compared to socio-economic and demographic measures, of which income is a major component. Indeed, the relatively minor health effects of risk factors have been known since the 1970s — a finding confirmed since then by many studies in Canada and elsewhere. This is especially the case for heart disease, adult-onset diabetes and respiratory disease.[19]

Social factors far outweigh risk factors in influencing health

Predictors	Life expectancy	Disability-free life expectancy	Fair or poor health
Socio-demographic factors	56%	32%	25%
Daily smoking rate	8%	6%	4%
Obesity rate	1%	5%	10%
Infrequent exercise rate	0%	3%	0%
Heavy drinking rate	1%	3%	1%
High stress rate	0%	0%	1%
Depression rate	0%	8%	9%

Note: Percentage of total variation (100%) in outcome predicted by each factor.
Source: M. Shields and S. Tremblay, 2002, "The Health of Canada's Communities," Health Reports, Supplement, 13(July): p. 1-22.

The focus on risk factors is clearly wrongheaded. Risk factors are not as important to health as risk conditions. To make matters worse, the emphasis on risk factors assumes all individuals are equally capable of making "healthy lifestyle choices," and that by failing to make these "choices" they bring on their own poor health. This process is known as "blaming the victim." Even if the people most vulnerable to poor health did make "healthy lifestyle choices" — and this is a big if, as behaviour change is difficult for everyone, especially stressed-out people experiencing disadvantage — it probably wouldn't make much of a difference in their health anyhow.

Despite all these problems, the risk factor approach dominates most government and public health activity and is the mainstay of disease-association communications (for example, from the

Heart and Stroke Foundation, Canadian Diabetes Association and Canadian Cancer Society). The media reinforce the risk factor understandings held by Canadians, thereby making communication of the risk condition analysis almost impossible.[20] Why should be we surprised then that governments feel no need to improve Canadians' living and working conditions?

WHAT ABOUT MEDICAL RESEARCH AND HEALTH CARE?

There is no doubt that profound improvements in health have occurred since 1900 in developed nations, including Canada. Most Canadians believe we now live longer lives because of the benefits of medical research and more advanced medical care. But researchers estimate that only 10–15 percent of the increased longevity in the last century is due to improved medical care. For example, vaccines, antibiotics and antitoxins are usually held responsible for the decline in mortality from infectious diseases in Canada since 1900. But dramatic declines in death from most causes had already occurred by the time Canadians were vaccinated for diseases such as measles, influenza and polio and receiving treatments for scarlet fever, typhoid and diphtheria.[21]

Medical care is important to Canadians, and proper care does much for the quality of life of those who are ill. But it does little to prevent disease in the first place. Most analysts conclude that improvements in health over the past century are due to improving material conditions of everyday life experienced by Canadians. The improvements came about in a long list of social determinants of health: living conditions during early childhood, education, food processing and availability, health and social services, housing, employment security and working conditions, among others. Citizen and labour movement activists have probably done more to improve Canadians' health than the medical and public health communities.[22]

SOCIAL DETERMINANTS OF HEALTH AND PUBLIC POLICY

It is clear that the SDoH are the primary causes of health and illness and that their unequal distribution is the best explanation for the profound health differences among groups of Canadians. These factors also explain how Canadians compare in health terms to residents of other nations. Canadians live longer and better than Americans but do not live as long or as well as Swedes. This has much to do with differences in public policy. Sweden, for example, makes sure that its residents are provided with economic and social security, making for better health. Canada does much less of this, and the United States does even less than we do.[23]

Most risk factor approaches to health and disease prevention also fail to take into account how experiences accumulate over time. Adults, and increasingly adolescents and children, are told that if they adopt a "healthy lifestyle" they will prevent chronic diseases such as heart disease, adult-onset diabetes and respiratory disease, among others. In contrast, the social determinants of health approach directs attention to how living conditions during pregnancy, childhood and adolescence not only immediately influence health but also form the basis for health or illness during later stages of life.[24]

Canada's market economy, as all capitalist market economies, plays a large role in determining health by shaping the distribution of income and wealth through employment and wages. This distribution plays a large part in whether Canadians can gain access — by having money to buy these things — to the SDoH, such as food, housing, education and so on.

How the social determinants of health get under our skin

Materialist explanation

The materialist framework sees objective living and working conditions as explaining how social determinants of health shape health outcomes. These experiences accumulate during our lives. There are three key mechanisms that link social determinants to health: 1. experience of actual health-enhancing or health-threatening living and working conditions; 2. extent of psycho-social stress associated with living and working conditions; and 3. adoption of health-supporting or health-threatening behaviours if living and working conditions are unfavourable and stressful.

Neo-materialist explanation

Neo-materialists share the concern about how health outcomes come to be associated with living and working conditions over the lifecourse, but extend the analysis to consider how health-advantaging or threatening living conditions come about. The focus is on how economic and social resources — the distribution of the social determinants of health — are allocated amongst the population. Generally, nations that distribute income and wealth more equitably also spend more on various aspects of social infrastructure that are associated with the social determinants of health. These nations usually have better health outcomes.

Psycho-social comparison explanation

In this model, material and social conditions of life are downplayed in favour of individuals' perception of their placement in the social hierarchy. In unequal societies, individuals compare their status and possessions to others and experience feelings of shame, worthlessness and envy, which have psycho-biological effects upon health. People who feel disadvantaged will also adopt health-threatening coping behaviours, such as overeating and tobacco and excessive alcohol use.

Adapted from D. Raphael, 2016, Social Determinants of Health: Canadian Perspectives, *third edition, Canadian Scholars' Press.*

Those who manage and profit from the market economy attempt to move more and more aspects of society into their sphere of operation. They do this because there are large profits to be made from shifting sectors that historically were considered part of the public domain — education, utilities, transportation, health care, housing, etc. — into the market economy. This shift is known as "privatization."

An associated process, "commodification," occurs when economic and social resources are privatized and must be purchased as commodities. When a society provides a resource as a matter of right, the resource is decommodified. Decommodification is especially important for health as it would allow access to many social determinants of health to people who are unable to work, or to find work, or who have wages too low to afford them. In Canada, decommodification has been primarily limited to education from kindergarten to secondary school, medically necessary procedures and library services, as well as basics such as police and fire protection and roads. In many nations, employment training, child-care, post-secondary education, dental and home-care are decommodified and considered public rights. Among developed nations, Canada is among the lowest in its decommodification of what citizens need to be healthy.

Canada's market economy is subject to minimal public control.

Few restrictions are placed on the ability of businesses to hire and fire, determine workers' levels of wages and benefits, and provide training and advancement to workers. The corporate and business sector has successfully moved several formerly public resources — such as medical services (for example, screening and lab testing, hospital cleaning), public resources (Petro Canada and Air Canada) and housing (government-provided social housing and co-ops) — into the private domain.

In his analysis of the harmful health effects of the market economy's unbridled operation in the U.K., Canada and the U.S., British sociologist Graham Scambler calls this form of the market economy "disorganized capitalism." Another apt term comes from sociologist Colin Leys, who talks about "market-driven politics" to explain how this uncontrolled market economy distorts public priorities. These developments are not good for health.[25]

Public policy decisions made by various levels of government have a strong impact on the social determinants of health. The impact results from governments deciding to intervene or not intervene in the market economy. For instance, the quality of early life will be shaped by whether or not parents have jobs that pay enough for adequate food and housing and educational opportunities, among others things, for their children. Governments can introduce public policies that assure that parents' have employment security, living wages, good quality working conditions and quality, regulated childcare. These are conditions or factors that for most people do not come under individual control; but they can be provided through public policy. Each and every social determinant of health can be made better or worse through public policy action.

To what extent does Canada's market economy allow us to experience the conditions necessary for health? And if the market economy does not meet these needs, to what extent do governments intervene — in the form of public policy — to provide us with these conditions?

Why do some nations gather and analyze information about the SDoH and use that knowledge to manage the economy and make public policy while others do not? The way a society chooses to provide citizens with various forms of security (such as income, employment, housing and food security, among others) is revealing and impactful.

SOCIAL INEQUALITIES

The social determinants of health influence all Canadians, but their effects are especially important for those experiencing the most material and social disadvantage. In Canada, these include people on lower incomes and those with less education. The people who are at greater social disadvantage also include Indigenous people, Canadians of colour (especially recent immigrants), women and persons with disabilities. The operation of Canada's market economy and governments' decisions to intervene or not intervene in it through public policy action can cause the SDoH to improve, stagnate or decline. If the process leads to stagnation or decline, it is these Canadians whose health is most at risk.

The more vulnerable Canadians are also the people with less power and ability to influence the public policy process. Indigenous people have less influence than non-Indigenous Canadians; women have less influence than men; Canadians of colour have less influence than white Canadians; newcomers have less influence than persons born in Canada; those with lower incomes and less wealth have less influence than those with greater incomes and wealth; and persons with disabilities have less influence than those without disabilities.

The term that describes these differences in status, influence and power is "social inequality."

Social inequality is closely related to health inequity. Health inequities can only be reduced in combination with reductions in social inequalities. Improving health is also about reducing the inequalities in power and influence among Canadians. Working towards a reduction in health and social inequities will require educating Canadians and building social and political movements in support of public policy that focuses not just on the social determinants of health but also on a more equitable distribution of power and influence.

2

LIVING CONDITIONS, STRESS AND THE HUMAN BODY

Stress carries several negative health consequences, including heart disease, stroke, high blood pressure, as well as immune and circulatory complications. Exposure to stress can also contribute to behaviours such as smoking, over-consumption of alcohol, and less-healthy eating habits.
— Statistics Canada[1]

If living and working conditions are the best predictors of health status and if their health effects swamp the influence of biomedical factors and health behaviours, how do these conditions — our early experiences, our income and our exposures to varying quality employment, food, housing and health care and social services — come to shape health? How do they get under our skin?

GETTING UNDER THE SKIN

The most common application of the focus on the social determinants of health is when health care providers and public health workers recognize that difficult living and working conditions make individuals more vulnerable to illness and injury and more likely to cope with stress by taking up health-threatening behaviours such as smoking and excessive alcohol use. They then target services toward Canadians who experience low income, insecure and low-wage employment, inadequate housing and food insecurity for health care services and behaviour modification programs. Making health care services more available to the vulnerable is a worthy effort. However, imposing behaviour modification programs upon the vulnerable in the mistaken belief that illness and injury will be prevented, without changing their living and working conditions, is not so worthy. The problem is that health care provision and behaviour modification programs are not concerned about how the SDoH directly affect health as well as contribute to the adoption of risk behaviours. These narrow efforts are also not concerned with improving the quality of the SDoH and making their distribution more equitable.

A focus on "pathways" links various SDoH directly and indirectly to health. The SDoH themselves are linked to the organization of society. In this pathways approach, "social structure" is composed of a society's economic system, government laws and regulations, and other major institutions and agencies, all influenced by business,

Failings of the lifestyle approach to health and illness

Lifestyle messaging essentially adds insult to injury for those Canadians most likely to experience poor health. The adverse living and working conditions that many Canadians experience are the primary causes of disease and illness, yet messaging about lifestyle attributes their health problems to their own behavioural choices. In other words: We will do nothing to improve your living and working conditions (injury), and we will now blame you for getting sick (insult).

labour and other interest groups. The social structure distributes material and social resources, thereby shaping living and working conditions.[2]

Three primary pathways link social structure with health in terms of well-being, morbidity and mortality. The first pathway is the direct material link between social structure and health. Material factors are the concrete living and working conditions that directly either enhance or threaten health. As examples, insecure and dangerous work creates stress and injuries; crowded housing breeds infections; and lack of food creates nutritional deficiencies.

The model links social structure to health and disease via material, psycho-social and behavioural pathways. Genetics, early life and cultural factors are further important influences upon population health.

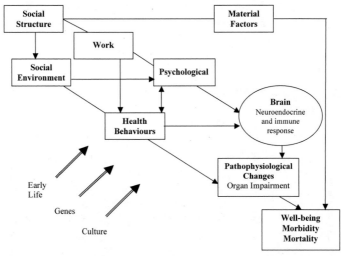

Source: E. Brunner and M.G. Marmot, "Social Organization, Stress, and Health," in M.G. Marmot and R.G. Wilkinson (eds.), Social Determinants of Health, *Oxford: Oxford University Press, Figure 2.2, p. 9, 2006.*

The second pathway involves social and work environments, which influence psychological states that go on to shape health. Psychological states that contribute to ill health include stress, a sense of lack of control and self-efficacy, and a perception that the world is not understandable or controllable. Social environments differ in their safety and security, their degree of intellectual and emotional support, and their threats, such as crime, family disorder and lack of role models. These differences in social environments result from the economic and social resources available to citizens, for example, access to child-care, affordable housing, community recreation facilities, public transportation, quality schools and responsive social and health care services. Social environments are strong social determinants of health.[3]

Work environments differ in their degree of security, the demands made upon workers and the amount of control workers have. They also offer different reward structures (i.e., wages, advancement opportunities, recognition). Work environments — like social

A sense of coherence is an important determinant of health

A sense of coherence ... is a mixture of optimism and control. It has three components – comprehensibility, manageability and meaningfulness. Comprehensibility is the extent to which events are perceived as making logical sense, that they are ordered, consistent and structured. Manageability is the extent to which a person feels they can cope. Meaningfulness is how much a person feels that life makes sense and challenges are worthy of commitment.

Source: J. Collingwood, 2013, Your Sense of Coherence, Psych Central <psychcentral.com/lib/your-sense-of-coherence/>.

environments — shape a number of psychological processes. This collection of psychological processes is referred to as a "sense of coherence" and it has been found to be a strong determinant of health.[4]

The third pathway links social and work environments to behavioural coping responses, such as tobacco use, excessive alcohol use and the adoption of carbohydrate-rich meals and a sedentary lifestyle, all of which can impair bodily functioning. Individuals experiencing material deprivation and the stress associated with deprivation not surprisingly cope in ways that may damage health.

MATERIAL LIVING CONDITIONS AND HEALTH

One way of thinking about this is that across the lifecourse an individual accumulates "income potential": the abilities, skills and educational experiences necessary for adult employability and income capacity. Education is key to this process and is strongly influenced by family circumstances during childhood. As a result of these experiences one also accumulates "health capital," which determines health during the early stages of life as well as in the future.[5]

STRESS AND HEALTH

The human fight or flight reaction evolved to deal with sudden and dangerous threats in the environment. That activation involves a number of bodily systems: the sympathetic and parasympathetic nervous systems, the neuro-endocrine system and the metabolic system. After the threat is passed, the systems return to their normal levels of functioning.

If the reaction is elicited in a chronic way as a response to continuing threats associated with social conditions such as low income, insecure employment, and housing and food insecurity, among others, the toll on health is substantial. Chronic fight or flight reaction weakens the immune system and disrupts the neuroendocrine and metabolic systems. The lived experience of low income, insecure employment, and housing and food insecurity is especially stressful. Individuals in difficult living circumstances experience a greater likelihood of neuroendocrine — nerve stimulation and hormone — disorders, such as adult-onset diabetes; autonomic and metabolic — nutrient processing and balance — disorders, such as heart disease and kidney failure; and weakened immunity to infections and disease.[6]

HEALTH RISK BEHAVIOURS AND HEALTH

The health-supporting or health-threatening behaviours that people adopt do have health consequences. But, individuals who experience difficult living conditions and high amounts of stress often

Angelica is Ojibwa and poor

In addition to being afflicted with PTSD and other psychiatric disorders, Angelica writes about a number of her debilitating physical illnesses — spinal stenosis, fibromyalgia, rheumatoid arthritis, diabetes, heart disease, incontinence (she often wears diapers, which give her rashes), and undiagnosed digestive distress that causes her to vomit — and how they connect to her experience of poverty.... her journal entries tells us: "they run hand in hand, so to speak. It's every day, sometimes it's bloody tough when you need to feed yourself properly to reduce the severity of symptoms [and it] is the time you've run out of soft food that you can swallow.... [Poverty] can also bring back memories of hunger, thirst, being so alone, shame I'm broke. Sometimes I've cried because of the other illness that I have."

Source: CCPA-Manitoba, 2009, It Takes All Day to Be Poor: State of the Inner City.

The psycho-biological stress response

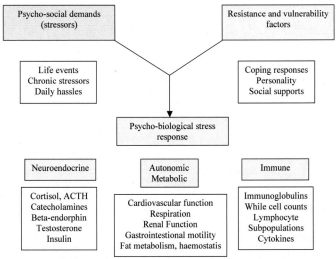

Source: E. Brunner and M.G. Marmot, "Social Organization, Stress, and Health." In M.G. Marmot and R.G. Wilkinson (eds.), Social Determinants of Health. Oxford: Oxford University Press, Figure 2.11, p. 27, 2006.

adopt "risk behaviours" as a means of coping with that stress. They are more likely to smoke tobacco and consume alcohol excessively than people whose lives are less stressful. They also find it difficult to eat nutritious diets and take up physical leisure activities.[7] Eating carbohydrate-dense diets and gaining weight, rather than being "unhealthy lifestyle choices," are more realistically seen as a coping response to difficult life circumstances. Mary Shaw and her colleagues at Bristol University put it this way:

> We also see that some of the factors which contribute to health inequalities — such as smoking and inadequate

diet — are themselves strongly influenced by the unequal distribution of income, wealth and life chances in general. These factors do not simply reflect the lack of knowledge or fecklessness of the poorer members of society.[8]

SOCIAL COMPARISON AND HEALTH

Some researchers take the "social comparison" approach to health, a theory which is usually presented as an alternative to explanations that focus on material living conditions. This explanation favours the view that an individual's perception of their place in the social hierarchy and the "social distance" between groups can explain health differences.[9]

Being poor is stressful

Tracey is a stay-at-home mother of two children. Her husband has a full-time minimum-wage job:

"We fit into the category of 'working poor.' We do not live from paycheque to paycheque — we live from payday to three days after payday, at best. Neither my friends nor my extended family fit into this category, nor do they realize that I do, thus I am constantly struggling to keep up the façade that I am financially okay. The truth is, I'm not. I'm poor. It is degrading and depressing.... I constantly worry about how I'm going to pay the bills, or what I'm going to do if one of our kids get sick and the prescription isn't covered, or what if there is a field trip at school and I don't have the extra money to send my child.... They say that money doesn't buy happiness. But it sure alleviates some of the stress that comes with being poor."

Source: K. Green, 2001, Telling it Like It Is: The Realities of Parenting in Poverty. *University of Saskatchewan, Department of Community Health and Epidemiology.*

This social comparison phenomenon occurs on two levels. At the individual level, unequal societies lead people to compare their status, possessions and other life circumstances to the situation of better-off others and experience feelings of shame, worthlessness and envy, which have psycho-biological effects upon their health. They make attempts to alleviate distress through overspending, taking on additional employment (which can threaten their health) and come to overeat and use alcohol and tobacco. At the communal level, inequality weakens social cohesion. As people become more distrusting and suspicious of others, those with more influence and power — and even those who would benefit from social programs that would support health, become critical of government actions such as universal provision of health care and affordable housing and daycare.

The social comparison explanation, however, neglects the profound and concrete health effects of material and social living conditions. The approach is especially problematic in the case of

Social and psychological deprivation equals poor health

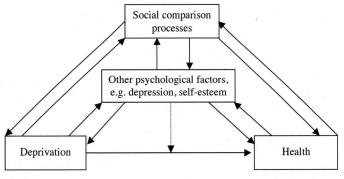

Source: E. Graham et al., 2000, "Individual Deprivation, Neighbourhood, and Recovery from Illness," in H. Graham (ed.), Understanding Health Inequalities, Open University Press.

people living in poverty, but it also ignores the growing material insecurity of many members of the middle class. The social comparison approach also does not consider political issues: namely, how societal resources are distributed and the political forces that shape these decisions. By stressing psychological processes, it directs attention away from the political, economic and social forces behind the issues related to the SDoH. Its emphasis on maladaptive coping on the part of people experiencing difficult living and working conditions can lead to "blaming the victim" rather than working to improve living and working conditions.

CHILD IS PARENT TO THE ADULT

How we live and work right now affects our current health, but it also affects our health later in life. These health effects can be latent, pathway and cumulative.[10]

Biological and social developmental experiences early in life can influence later health, particularly when they happen in sensitive development periods. Pregnancy is one of the most sensitive of those periods when latent effects occur. The quality of nutrients that the mother receives, the incidence of infection, the presence of stress, and the use of alcohol and tobacco all affect the availability of oxygen to organs. These latent effects come to affect blood clotting and cholesterol metabolism, leading to coronary heart disease and adult-onset diabetes in later life.

A child experiencing malnutrition and infections during infancy and early childhood can also experience latent effects. Malnutrition influences cognitive and emotional development, educational attainment during childhood and later life, and physical and mental health. Infections lead to long-term developmental risk and increased likelihood of heart disease and respiratory disease.[11]

"Pathway" effects refer to experiences that set individuals on trajectories that eventually come to influence health over the life-course. Parents' living and working conditions, for example, shape the vocabularies children have when they enter school. This contingency sets them upon a path that leads to differing education expectations and achievement, employment prospects, greater or lesser accumulation of financial resources, and a likelihood of either avoiding or developing a range of diseases across the lifespan. The material and social conditions associated with neighbourhoods, schools and housing of varying quality also set children on differing paths, which either support or threaten health across the lifespan. Early life may therefore be a particularly critical or sensitive period in itself, or it may set a path that a person takes through the rest of life. In both cases children accumulate experiences that lead to health or illness.[12]

"Cumulative effects" are the combination of latent and pathway effects that accumulate as advantage or disadvantage over time. If children escape disadvantage, the accumulation of disadvantage stops, but the previously accumulated health disadvantage continues with them into adulthood.

SOCIAL FORCES LEAD TO DIFFERING LIVING AND WORKING CONDITIONS

The quality and distribution of the social determinants of health are important for health. But, how do those living and working conditions — as either advantage or threat to health — come about? In general, they are the result of how socio-political decisions are made of how to allocate economic and social resources among Canadians.

In some nations the quality and distribution of the SDoH is such that there is an advantageous effect for a large proportion of the population, but in other nations there is a much less satisfactory result.

Why do nations that distribute income and wealth more equitably also have higher standards for the delivery of the other SDoH to their population?

Canada has a less skewed distribution of income and wealth than the United States, and not surprisingly, we enjoy generally better health than do residents of the U.S. Our infant mortality rates are lower, life expectancy is higher and incidence of, and mortality from, a range of diseases and childhood and adult injuries is lower. Still, our health indicators are not as good as those of many European nations. Especially compared to Scandinavian countries, where the quality of the SDoH is better and their distribution more equitable, we lag well behind on infant mortality rates, for example.[13]

Links have been made between the political and economic approaches of nations and how they address the SDoH. Nations that allow the market economy — as opposed to government regulation of the market economy — to determine the distribution of resources, tend to have a more unequal distribution of income and wealth. They also tend to have fewer and lower quality public supports to citizens in the form of benefits, programs and services, all of which influence the quality and distribution of other SDoH. Much of this is driven by the political ideology followed by a nation's ruling authorities and leaders, sometimes but not always with the support of its population. Since the 1980s, Canadian authorities have adopted the ideology of neoliberalism, which has profoundly shaped public policy approaches in a variety of areas related to the quality and distribution of the SDoH.[14]

The belief that the marketplace should determine how economic and other resources are organized and distributed limits the role of government in a wide range of areas. Neoliberal oriented-governments are less likely to take action to strengthen the overall quality and equitable distribution of the SDoH. Neoliberal governments give businesses the go-ahead to do whatever they wish, which translates for many into insecure and low-paying employment. This is part of the process of economic globalization, which has adverse effects upon the lives of average Canadians. The key impact is that well-paying industrial jobs have been moved away from Canada, most often to low-wage, low-regulation jurisdictions.[15]

Canadian sociologist David Coburn maps out the relationships between economic globalization and both neoliberalism and the political power of the corporate sector (through lobbying governments) to shape public policy that affects the SDoH. As neoliberalism and corporate interests expand, the welfare state is cut back and public supports are replaced by the market. This withdrawal leads to increasing income inequality, continuing high levels of poverty and stagnating or declining governmental expenditures on SDoH such as education, housing, early child development,

Neoliberalism: Letting the market rule

Neoliberalism refers to the dominance of markets in society. It has the following tenets:

- markets are the best and most efficient producers and allocators of resources;
- societies are composed of autonomous individuals (producers and consumers) motivated chiefly or entirely by material or economic considerations; and
- competition is the major market vehicle for innovations.
- The essence of neoliberalism is a more-or-less thoroughgoing adherence, in rhetoric if not in practice, to the virtues of a market economy and, by extension, a market-oriented society.

Source: Adapted from D. Coburn, 2000, "Income Inequality, Social Cohesion, and the Health Status of Populations: The Role of Neoliberalism," Social Science and Medicine 51.

health care and social services. The end result of these public policy approaches is declining quality of health and well-being.[16]

WELFARE STATES AND THE SOCIAL DETERMINANTS OF HEALTH

Nations that have developed more equity-oriented approaches to providing citizens with economic and social security are more willing to resist neoliberal pressures. European nations in general have resisted to a far greater extent than North American nations the demands of the business sector to deregulate industry. Their public policy focus on equality, equity and social rights is related to vigorous approaches to promoting health and well-being. In contrast, countries like Australia, Canada, the U.S., the U.K. and Ireland, called liberal

Increased power of corporations means poorer health and well-being

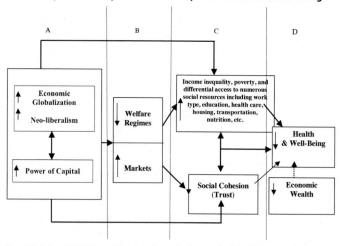

Source: D. Coburn, 2004, "Beyond the Income Inequality Hypothesis: Globalization, Neo-Liberalism, and Health Inequalities," Social Science & Medicine 58.

welfare states, provide the least support and security to their citizens. The policy profiles of Canada and the U.K. are consistently found to be closer to that of the U.S. than to European social democratic and conservative welfare states, where citizen security and support are more ensured.[17]

Liberal welfare states champion liberty, which is interpreted as minimal government intervention in the marketplace. Indeed, government interventions are seen as providing a disincentive to work, thereby breeding what is often called "welfare dependence." The results are the meagre benefits provided to those on social assistance in the U.S., Canada and the U.K., generally weaker legislative support for the labour movement, underdeveloped policies for assisting those with disabilities and a reluctance to provide universal services and

Liberal welfare states provide the least for citizens

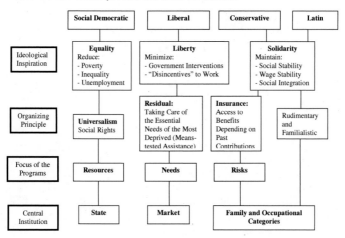

Source: S. Saint-Arnaud and P. Bernard, 2003, "Convergence or Resilience? A Hierarchical Cluster Analysis of the Welfare Regimes in Advanced Countries," Current Sociology 51 (5).

programs. The programs that exist are "residual," meaning they exist to provide the most basic needs of the most deprived.

Liberal welfare states represent the interests of those allied with the central institution of these nations: the market. It is no accident that liberal welfare states have the greatest degree of wealth and income inequality, the weakest safety nets and the poorest performance on indicators of population health, such as infant mortality and life expectancy. These states' public policy-makers are especially responsive to the interests of the business sector, and the business sectors in the U.S., Canada and the U.K. are opposed to policies that would reduce social inequality by more equitably distributing income and wealth and strengthening the welfare state through the provision of universal benefits.[18]

Social democratic welfare states exemplify the opposite situation. For these nations, the state is a form of collective responsibility, and it aims for the reduction of poverty, inequality and unemployment. Rather than seeing government responsibility as being limited to meeting the most basic needs of the most deprived, the organizing principle is universalism and provision for the social rights of all

Liberal welfare states do not support the SDoH

The liberal welfare state provides fewer economic and social supports for the population, universal benefits are sparse, and state provision of modest benefits is targeted at the least well-off. Organizing the workplace is difficult such that collective agreements are less likely and the distribution of wages and benefits more skewed. As a result, the distribution of income — as well as SDoH associated with income, such as housing and food security — is more problematic in liberal welfare states.

citizens. Denmark, Finland, Norway and Sweden are the best exemplars of this form of the welfare state.

Governments with social democratic political economies are proactive in identifying social problems and issues. They strive to promote citizens' economic and social security. These welfare states have come closest to the elimination of poverty, striving for gender and social class equity and regulation of the market in the service of citizens. They have notable public policy programs that serve to reduce social inequality, such as child-care, supports for people with disabilities, actions against racism and homophobia, provision of employment training and quality education.[19]

Even the so-called conservative (Belgium, France, Germany, Netherlands) and Latin (Greece, Italy, Portugal, Spain) welfare states generally provide superior economic and social security to their citizens as compared to liberal welfare states. The goals of social stability, wage stability and social integration are accomplished through benefits based on insurance schemes geared to sustaining the family. These well-organized benefits schemes are directed towards the primary wage-earners with rather less concern for promoting gender equity than is the case among social democratic nations.

Despite some debate about which countries fall into these categories, it is clear that the Nordic nations of Finland, Denmark, Sweden and Norway are the representative social democratic states, and Canada, the U.K. and the U.S. are the liberal states. In any case, the SDoH are shaped by approaches to public policy. Governments need to do whatever they can to strengthen the SDoH and make their distribution more equitable if they are truly concerned about the health of their citizens.[20]

INCOME, EDUCATION AND WORK

Health status improves at each step up the income and social hierarchy. High income determines living conditions such as safe housing and ability to buy sufficient good food. The healthiest populations are those in societies which are prosperous and have an equitable distribution of wealth.
— Public Health Agency of Canada[1]

F our especially important social determinants of health — income, education, employment security and working conditions — are inter-related. They shape the material conditions of daily life, psychological functioning and the extent to which people refrain from health-damaging coping behaviours. In addition, the economic resources available to individuals and families shape the quality of other SDoH, such as early child development, food security, housing and the experience of social exclusion. This is because, in Canada, employment in the marketplace is the primary source of people's financial resources.

In societies where governments do not enact laws and regulations to ensure employment security, good wages, benefits and working conditions, and easy organization of workforces into unions, the distribution of these important SDoH is very poor. Since Canada is a nation where governments weakly manage the workplace, there is great variation in living and working conditions. These differences in conditions lead to the profound health inequities we see among Canadians.

In Canada, employment security, wages and benefits depend more upon a person's social-class background and educational attainment than on workplace laws and regulations that apply to all workers. As a result, Canada falls among a group of wealthy developed nations with the highest rates of income inequality and poverty, and the greatest proportions of low-waged workers and employment insecurity. Canada is also among the most frugal wealthy developed nations in its level of income-related benefits such as family benefits, social assistance levels and unemployment benefits. All of these factors contribute to inequities in health.

INCOME AND HEALTH

Income is likely the most important social determinant of health. It is usually thought of in two different but related ways. First, there is the actual amount of income received by an individual or family — *income available* is an excellent indicator of the health of individuals and families. The second way looks at the distribution of income across the population. This provides a measure of the distribution of economic resources and describes the gap between rich and poor. *Income inequality* is one of the best predictors of the overall health of a society, although there is debate about why this is the case.[2]

An individual's or family's income affects overall living conditions and psychological functioning and determines in large part health-related behaviours such as quality of diet, extent of physical activity, tobacco use and excessive alcohol use. Income also determines the quality of other social determinants of health such as food and housing security, early child development and extent of social exclusion.

Income is even more important in nations like Canada that provide fewer benefits and services as a matter of citizen rights. In Canada, public education until Grade 12, medically necessary procedures and libraries are funded from general revenues, but child-care, dental care, housing, post-secondary education, recreational opportunities and resources for retirement are for the most part commodified: individuals must pay for them. In contrast, many wealthy developed nations provide child-care, child benefits, housing support, employment training and tuition-free post-secondary education as citizen rights. Public pensions in most other wealthy developed nations are also more generous than they are in Canada.[3]

Individuals and families with lower incomes experience more health problems. The lower the income, the less likely it is that individuals and families have access to good quality healthy levels of food, clothing and housing. Lower income Canadians are also excluded from participating in the cultural, educational and recreational activities expected of citizens in advanced wealthy nations. As mentioned in Chapter 1, the distribution of income and economic resources is known as the social gradient in health.[4]

Dr. Nathalie Auger and Carolyne Alix of the Quebec Ministry of Health demonstrate how a neighbourhood material deprivation index — with income being a key element — is related to health outcomes in Quebec. The neighbourhood index is based on income, education and employment, which is then related to average life expectancy in each neighbourhood. These patterns are illustrative of those discussed in Chapter 1 for Canada as a whole.

In Quebec, men living in the most deprived neighbourhoods live almost four years less than those in the most advantaged areas.

Poor people die at much higher rates than wealthy people

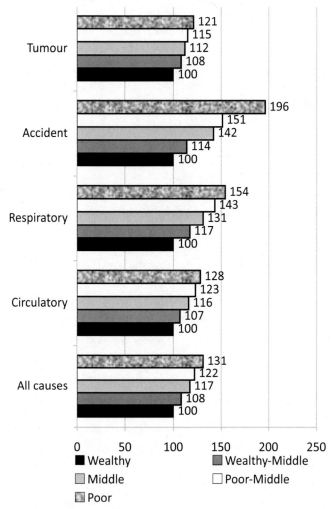

Source: N. Auger and C. Alix, 2016, "Income, Income Distribution, and Health in Canada," in D. Raphael (ed.), Social Determinants of Health: Canadian Perspectives, *third edition, Canadian Scholars' Press.*

For women the difference is almost three years less. Infant mortality rates follow roughly the same pattern. Infant mortality is said to be an especially sensitive indicator of societal health, and the rates in the most deprived Quebec neighbourhoods are 30 percent higher (6.0/1000) than in the wealthiest areas (4.6/1000).

Moreover, death rates from a variety of afflictions are also a function of neighbourhood deprivation. Those living in the most deprived neighbourhoods had death rates that were 31 percent higher than people in the least deprived neighbourhoods. In terms of respiratory disease, the rates in the most deprived neighbourhoods were 54 percent higher than in the least deprived. Death rates from circulatory diseases, accidents and tumours, not surprisingly, were similar. Suicide rates also differ as a function of neighbourhood income. The annual suicide rates in the most deprived neighbour-hoods in 2004–08 were almost twice (20.9/100,000) those seen in the wealthiest neighbourhoods (10.8/100,000).[5]

Most of these income-related differences cannot be accounted for by risk behaviours such as smoking and physical inactivity. In Saskatchewan, for example, lower income men and women are almost four times more likely than wealthy men and women to report having heart disease. More importantly, income was still an important pre-dictor of heart disease even after controlling for a range of behavioural factors. The authors of the study concluded:

> Low income had a more important association with heart disease than conventional risk factors such as smoking and physical inactivity ... [After controlling for such factors], lower-income residents were still 52 percent more likely to have heart disease than higher-income residents were. This suggests that a re-ordering of risk factors is required.[6]

Similarly, household income is the best predictor of both the percentage of Canadians with adult-onset diabetes and new cases of it each year. Men whose family income was at poverty levels (<$15,000) were twice as likely to have diabetes as wealthy men (>$80,000). Even taking into account education, weight and physical activity, this greater risk was only reduced from 207 to 194 percent. For women living in poverty, the corresponding greater risk of diabetes is 357 percent, and it is reduced to 275 percent by controlling for all these other factors. Developing diabetes over time follows a similar pattern. Ever having lived in poverty during a twelve-year period had a 41 percent greater chance of developing diabetes than those who never lived in poverty. Taking into account obesity and lack of physical inactivity only reduced this 41 percent greater risk to 36 percent.[7]

Poor people are more likely to have heart disease

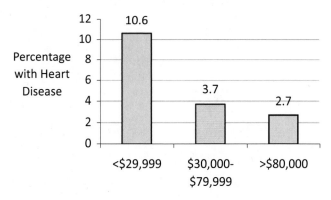

Source: Adapted from M. Lemstra et al., 2015, "Income and Heart Disease: Neglected Risk Factor," Canadian Family Physician 61 (12).

A Toronto study looked at three key indicators of children's health and well-being as a function of average neighbourhood income: low birth weight for births of a single child (excluding multiple births), readiness to learn at age of school entry and teen live births. For each indicator, the health outcomes are worse when the income of the neighbourhood is lower. Several other studies looking at a range of health indicators for children have found similar profound differences as a function of income.[8]

Clearly, low income is a health risk condition, more so than the health-related behaviours of diet, physical activity and even tobacco use. This means that income inequality and the material and social resources associated with income differences are the key health policy issues that need to be addressed by governments and policy-makers.

Have health gaps by income changed in Canada?

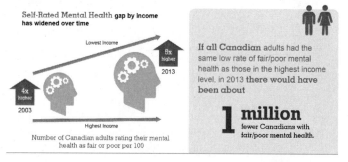

Self-Rated Mental Health gap by income has widened over time

Lowest Income

8x higher
2013

4x higher
2003

Highest Income

Number of Canadian adults rating their mental health as fair or poor per 100

If all Canadian adults had the same low rate of fair/poor mental health as those in the highest income level, in 2013 there would have been about

1 million
fewer Canadians with fair/poor mental health.

© 2015 Canadian Institute for Health Information

Canadian Institute for Health Information
Institut canadien d'information sur la santé

INCOME AND ITS DISTRIBUTION IN CANADA

A 2008 report by the Organisation for Economic Co-operation and Development (OECD) identified Canada as one of two wealthy developed nations (among thirty) that showed the greatest increases in income inequality and poverty from the 1990s to the mid-2000s. Since then the growth in inequality has levelled off and Canada is now close to the OECD average. In the mid-1980s, Canada's score was .28 (on the Gini coefficient measure of income equality), which

The rich are getting richer and the poor are getting poorer

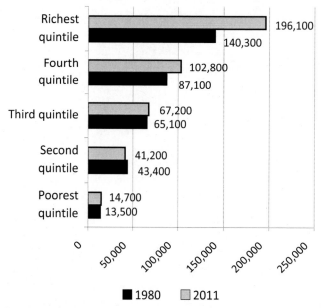

Source: A. Curry-Stevens, 2016, "Precarious Changes: A Generational Exploration of Canadian Incomes and Wealth," in D. Raphael (ed.), Social Determinants of Health: Canadian Perspectives, *third edition, Canadian Scholars' Press.*

gave it a rank of eleventh among twenty-one nations for which data were available. Now, with a score of .31, we are ranked twentieth of thirty-four OECD nations.[9]

Ann Curry-Stevens, a Canadian working at Portland State University, shows that from 1980 to 2011, the bottom 60 percent of Canadian families experienced virtually no increase in market incomes in constant dollars, while the top 20 percent of Canadian families did very well (increasing by over 37 percent). Increases in income inequality have led to what's known as a "hollowing out" of the middle class in Canada. Significant increases from 1980 to 2011 in the percentages of Canadian families who were either poor or very rich means that there are now fewer Canadian families who earn middle-level incomes.

Of even more concern — considering that Canada entered a long recession in 2008 — is that income inequality increases dramatically during periods of economic recession and recovery. During the recessions of 1981–84 and 1989–93, the market incomes of the bottom 20 percent of Canadians declined by 45 percent and 60 percent, respectively, while the decline for the top 20 percent of income-earners was 5 percent and 7 percent. However, during recoveries from the two earlier recessions, the bottom 20 percent of income-earners saw their incomes increase by only $2,975 and $1,260, respectively; the corresponding increases for the top 20 percent of income-earners were $14,460 and $12,030.

The increases in wealth inequality in Canada are even more troubling. Wealth is probably a better indicator of long-term health outcomes because it is a more sensitive measure of financial security than is income. From the period of 1999 to 2012, the bottom 20 percent of Canadian families on average had virtually no net worth ($1,000), and over this period their net worth declined. In contrast, the net worth of the top 20 percent of Canadian families in 2012 was $1.4 million, an increase of $616,000 in constant dollars from 1999. The next highest 20 percent of families' net worth in 2012 was $575,000, representing an increase of $262,000 since 1999.[10]

EDUCATION AND HEALTH

Education is an important social determinant of health. Canadians of higher educational attainment are healthier than those of lower attainment.[11] An important question is whether or not it is education that causes better health or whether it serves as a means of achieving greater material and social resources. It is probably both. The level of education attained is highly correlated with levels of income, employment security and better working conditions — all of which are themselves important social determinants of health.

Education is also one way in which the employment marketplace stratifies individuals, setting those with lesser education on the path to health-threatening social conditions. If health-sustaining wages and benefits and necessary services such as affordable child-care and housing were available to all, lower educational attainment would in all likelihood become a less important marker of disadvantage in Canada.[12]

At a societal level, a more educated population is better able to respond to challenges related to changing economic and social conditions. Being better educated makes it more likely that individuals will be able to benefit from occupational training opportunities, and from retraining too if employment situations change. Being better educated usually facilitates citizen engagement in the political process. All of this should lead to a healthier population.

Greater literacy is associated with a better understanding of health and the factors that improve health, linking education to good health more closely than as a precursor to improved economic circumstances. Health literacy influences the extent to which individuals promote their own health and the health of those around them. Also, having greater general literacy is related to having a greater understanding of the world and of how to at least attempt to influence what is going on. The sense of coherence gained from literacy is strongly related to better health.

THE STATE OF EDUCATION

Charles Ungerleider, formerly of the University of British Columbia, and Tracey Burns, of the Organisation for Economic Cooperation and Development, point out that Canadian children fare well in international assessments of reading, science and mathematics achievement. Among the wealthy developed nations of the OECD, Canada has one of the highest proportions (53 percent) of its population with some post-secondary education. But disparities exist among certain populations and regions, and these differences "do not seem to be diminishing with time." Lower socio-economic status and second-language students perform less well than students who are more advantaged.[13]

On a positive note, immigrant children and children of immigrants in Canada do better than immigrant children and children of immigrants in other nations. In fact they do better than Canadian-born children of Canadian-born parents. Indeed, among nations participating in testing carried out through the OECD Programme for International Student Testing, Canadian students were some of the best in science, reading and mathematics.[14]

However, as Barbara Ronson McNichol and Irving Rootman point out, the OECD's Adult Literacy and Life Skills Survey found that young Canadians whose parents graduated from high school scored twenty-four points better on prose and document literacy than did those whose parents had only eight years of education. In contrast, the situation in Norway saw spreads of only thirteen points for these differing groups of children. This indicates that nations with well-developed welfare states weaken these parent education–child literacy relationships. Indeed, Swedish children not only outperform all other nations' children in prose, document and quantitative literacy, but Swedish children whose parents did not complete secondary school usually outperform children from other nations — including Canada — whose parents did complete secondary school.[15]

EMPLOYMENT AND HEALTH

Employment obviously provides income, but it also provides a sense of identity and well-being, and it helps people to structure day-to-day life. The lack of employment is associated with a host of physical and mental health problems that include depression, anxiety and increased suicide rates.

Mel Bartley, of University College London, outlines the mechanisms by which unemployment is related to health. First, unemployment leads to material deprivation and possibly poverty. Unemployment not only reduces income but often also removes benefits plans that come with jobs. Both are associated with increased likelihood of financial problems and have strong effects on health. Second, unemployment is a stressful event that is associated with a lowering of self-esteem, a loss of daily structure and routine, and increases in chronic anxiety. Third, unemployment leads to a greater incidence of adverse health-related coping behaviours, such as tobacco use and problem drinking.[16]

Employment insecurity has been on the increase in Canada, as Diane-Gabrielle Tremblay, of the Télè-Université of the Université du

Economic recession fuels suicide

"Alberta's suicide rate has grown almost 30 per cent in the first half of this year, compared to the same period last year... 'It says something really about the horrible human impact of what's happening in the economy with the recession,' counsellor David Kirby told CBC News. Kirby noted that demand for the Calgary Distress Centre's counselling services have gone up almost 80 per cent. Homicide rates have also increased over the past year, according to the Edmonton Journal."

Source: S. Rieger, 2015, "Alberta's Suicide Rate Spikes As Unemployment Soars." Huffington Post Alberta, December 7 <huffingtonpost.ca/2015/12/08/alberta-suicide-rate_n_8740202.html>.

Québec à Montréal, documents. Only about 50 percent of Canadian workers have a single full-time job that had been held for six months or more. Some 14 percent of Canadian workers were self-employed, 10 percent worked temporary jobs, and 18 percent worked part-time; 6 percent had been working in their current employment for less than six months; and 5 percent worked more than one job.[17]

Precarious work is associated with greater employment uncertainty, greater stress and lack of control at work. The increase in precarious work has also translated into a greater number of "working poor," the proportion increasing from 6 percent in 1975 to 8 percent in 2010. Dr. Emile Tompa, of the Institute for Work and Health in Toronto, and his colleagues show how the percentage of Canadians engaged in part-time work expanded — and this was particularly the case for the youngest- and oldest-aged groups. They argue that this trend is associated with intensification of work, increased insecurity, and stagnation and polarization of incomes.[18]

All of these are important predictors of adverse health outcomes.

New employment reality: Precarious jobs are stress-creating jobs

Precarious jobs don't have:

- Degree of certainty of continuing work
- Control over work processes
- Legal and institutional protection
- Income and benefits adequacy
- Work-role status
- Social support at work
- Training and career-advancement opportunities

Precarious jobs do have:

- Risk of exposure to physical hazards

Source: E. Tompa et al., 2007, "Precarious Employment Experiences and Their Health Consequences: Towards a Theoretical Framework," Work 28 (7).

Insecure employment is usually intensified work and is associated with higher rates of stress, injuries, and back, neck, and shoulder pain. Some studies find that the intensification of work is associated with headaches, sore muscles, fatigue, and nausea.[19]

Non-standard work hours are also unhealthy. Excessive hours of work cause physiological and psychological health problems, such as elevated blood pressure and coronary heart disease. Precarious work arrangements are associated with a variety of physical and mental health problems, such as stress, anxiety, pain and fatigue. One aspect of increasing job insecurity is downsizing, which has been associated with increased workplace fatalities, workplace accidents, musculo-skeletal injuries and psychiatric disorders. Perceived job insecurity has negative effects on marital relationships, parenting effectiveness and children's behaviour.[20]

WORKING CONDITIONS AND HEALTH

Working conditions are of crucial importance because the experience of work dominates most Canadians' lives. Those Canadians who are already most vulnerable to poor health outcomes due to their lower incomes and education are also the ones most likely to experience adverse working conditions, which further threaten their health. The title of an article by Andrew Jackson, of the Broadbent Institute, and Govind Rao, of the Canadian Union of Public Employees — "The Unhealthy Canadian Workplace" — makes the point succinctly.[21]

At the very minimum, work provides people with the necessary income and benefits that have an impact on health. But, several other dimensions of work also affect health outcomes: for example, job and employment security, physical conditions at work, work pace and stress, working time, opportunities for self-expression and individual development at work, participation in work, and work-life balance.

Peter Smith, of the Institute for Work and Health in Toronto, and Michael Polanyi describe two important ways in which workplace conditions also shape health outcomes. They call the first dynamic "effort-reward imbalance." The degree of incongruence between employee effort in response to demand (for example, time pressures, interruptions, responsibility, pressure to work overtime) and employee reward (monetary, esteem, respect from supervisors and colleagues) is reflected in health problems. When workers perceive that their efforts are not being adequately rewarded, they are more likely to develop a range of illnesses, afflictions and problems that include heart disease, hypertension, sleep disorders and anxiety disorders.

The second dynamic is called "job strain." Jobs can be classified along two dimensions: high control versus low control, and high demand versus low demand. Jobs that are especially related to adverse health outcomes are those in which workers have high demands made upon them but have little control over how these demands can be met. Of the two dimensions, control seems to be the most important: less control is related to more harmful health outcomes.[22]

Most people believe that professionals — such as corporate managers, lawyers, teachers and university professors — have the highest demands and that their jobs are therefore dangerous to health. But unlike those in working-class jobs, these people have more control over the various ways of coping with the stress — from time management to self-determined vacations. It is the lack of control — which is much more prevalent in working-class jobs — that is the greatest threat to health. Andrew Jackson points out:

> High demand/low control jobs have been found to be a significant contributing factor to high blood pressure, cardiovascular diseases, mental illness, and long-onset disability. Workers in high [high demand/low control] jobs are about twice as likely to experience depression as other workers of the same age and socioeconomic status with the same social supports. There is a link between low levels of control over working conditions to stress as well as to higher rates of work injuries. Even where work is physically demanding, there is less risk of injury if workers can vary the pace of work, take breaks when needed, and have some say in the design of workstations.[23]

Stress from high demand/low control jobs is more common among Canadian women than men. Statistics Canada found that 28 percent of women had these kinds of jobs, compared to 20 percent of men. These jobs are common among low-income sales and services workers.

Jackson and Rao note that over one-third of Canadian workers (35 percent) reported experiencing work-related stress from "too many demands or too many hours," up from 27.5 percent in 1991. Another survey found in 2005 that one in three workers (32.4 percent) reported that most days at work were stressful. Women scored higher (37 percent) than did men (32 percent) on "too many hours or too many demands."

In 1994 just four in ten Canadian workers said that they had a lot of freedom regarding work conditions and practices, which Jackson points out is much lower than the 54 percent in 1989. Men have more control over work (43 percent) than women (38 percent) do, and professionals and managers (51 percent) report more control than do skilled workers (35 percent) and unskilled workers (35 percent). Jackson and Rao conclude: "While we lack detailed information on changes in the overall incidence of work involving high demands and low worker control, high-stress work is common and likely on the increase."

There was also a strong trend to long (and short) working hours for men and women during the 1980s and 1990s. The percentage of men aged 25–54 who work more than fifty hours a week rose from 15 percent in the early 1980s to about 20 percent in 2006; for women the figures for more than fifty hours were 5 percent and 7 percent. About 33 percent of men and 12 percent of women now work more than forty-one hours per week. Jackson and Rao note that the shift to long daily and weekly hours is notably different in Canada and the United States as compared to continental Europe: "The usual weekly hours of full-time paid workers in the E.U. are below 40, and falling. Some countries, notably France, the Netherlands, and Germany, are now close to a 35-hour norm. The proportion of men working weekly hours much in excess of 40 hours is generally very low."

Other dimensions of the workplace that have been related to health outcomes are organizational justice, work hours, work–life conflict, precarious work and status inconsistency. All of these dimensions are related to the amount of influence and control that workers have in their workplaces. These conditions are clearly amenable to regulations and laws that would promote greater worker influence. Unionized workplaces that provide collective agreements are more likely to be able to put such changes into effect.

A great many workers face problems related to job insecurity. For example, the true unemployment rate is probably double the official one, 6.8 percent in April 2015. Canadians who are unemployed usually cycle in and out of employment. Precarious work is more widespread in Canada than elsewhere. European Union data provides evidence of increasing intensity of work and declining worker control over the workplace. In terms of Canada, Jackson and Rao state:

> Comparable data on the physical demands of work are simply unavailable for Canada, though one recent Canadian survey suggests that the incidence of high speed work in Canada and the U.S. is well above the average of all advanced industrial countries. There is little reason to believe that the situation here is any better than in the E.U.

The effects of job insecurity are heightened by the difficulty that many people have in getting access to Employment Insurance. Punitive and minimal social assistance programs make *any* job look attractive, and the precarious jobs that are available are frequently without benefits, such as drug, supplemental health, dental and pensions. Jackson and Rao state: "A large minority of workers experience continuing precarious employment and a significant risk of periodic unemployment. The risks to health of precarious employment caused by stress and anxiety are compounded by lack of access to benefits."[24]

One of the most obvious health–work connections is death and injury at the job. Workplace fatalities continue to be on the increase in Canada. The Association of Workers' Compensation Boards of Canada reports that in 2014, 919 workplace deaths were recorded in Canada— more than 2.5 deaths every single day. In addition, there were 239,643 claims accepted for lost time due to a work-related injury or disease.[25]

Yet these reports by workplaces of work-related injuries (often called "accidents") appear to be declining. However, workplace injuries are seriously underreported because both employers and employees face significant costs in reporting these accidents. While larger unionized workplaces usually emphasize safety, smaller non-unionized workplaces may not. The shift of employment to contracted-out smaller workplaces therefore bodes poorly for pre- venting workplace injuries.

Jackson and Rao also note apparent increases in repetitive strain and other soft tissue injuries in Canada, along with musculoskeletal pain and chronic back problems. These illnesses take time to appear and workers' compensation programs do a poor job of providing benefits for these types of problems. Jackson and Rao point out that 31 percent of Canadian workers believe that their employment puts their health and safety at risk — a figure that is slightly above the average for advanced industrial countries.[26]

Based on information about 2.7 million Canadians over sixteen years, Statistics Canada calculated death rates as a function of the person's income. Comparing the number of deaths of the wealthiest 20 percent to the other 80 percent of Canadians, if all Canadians were as healthy as the top 20 percent of income earners, there would be approximately 40,000 fewer deaths each year, every year. Of these, 25,000 fewer deaths would be among Canadian men and 15,000 among Canadian women.

Stated another way, in terms of the relative rate of mortality, a man in the poorest 20 percent group of Canadians has a 67 percent and a woman in the poorest 20 percent group of Canadians has a 52 percent greater chance of dying each year than their wealthy counterparts (relative mortality rates of 1.67 and 1.52). That's an excess death rate of 19.4 percent for men and 16.6 percent for women.

Moreover, poor Canadian males have a 63 percent greater chance

Source: D. Raphael and T. Bryant, 2014, "The Health Effects of Income Inequality: A Jet with 110 Canadians Falling Out of the Sky Each Day, Every Day, 365 Days a Year" <http://www.thinkupstream. net/health_effects_of_income_inequality>, based on data in M. Tjepkema, R. Wilkins and A. Long, 2013, "Cause-Specific Mortality by Income Adequacy in Canada: A 16-Year Follow-Up Study," Health Reports 24 (7): 14–22. Reprinted with permission of Upstream <thinkupstream.net>.

of dying each year from heart disease than their wealthy counterparts. For women it's a difference of 53 percent. Poor men have a 150 percent greater chance and poor women a 160 percent greater chance of dying from diabetes than wealthy Canadians!

This means that if all Canadians were as healthy as wealthy Canadians, there would be nearly 40 percent fewer deaths from diabetes and nearly 20 percent fewer deaths from cardiovascular disease every year. Similar numbers showing a profound difference between wealthy and poor Canadians and a still significant difference between wealthy and all other Canadians appear for virtually every known disease that can kill Canadians, including cancer, respiratory disease, injuries, HIV-AIDS and many more.[27]

MORE INCOME AND EMPLOYMENT EQUALITY EQUALS BETTER HEALTH

In Canada the quality of these key social determinants of health is either declining or stagnating. While Canadian children do very well in educational achievement, persistent educational attainment differences remain among groups in Canada. Of much more concern is the growing income and wealth inequality. Poverty levels are virtually unchanged from twenty years ago, but the growing inequalities in income and wealth suggest that those already disadvantaged will face even greater challenges in participating in society and maintaining their health than may have been the case in the past.

Additionally, the rise in employment insecurity and evidence of stagnating or worsening working conditions are causes for great concern. Precarious and low-waged employment is on the increase, which can only mean poorer health for more Canadians in the future. Many of these developments are related to growing inequalities in power and influence in the employment marketplace and workplace.

Average Canadians have less influence with governments and policy-makers than do those at the top of the economic ladder. The result is growing inequality and stagnating wages for most Canadians. If we are to change these conditions, governments must take steps to make it easier for workers to unionize and negotiate collective agreements.

EARLY CHILD DEVELOPMENT, FOOD SECURITY AND HOUSING

A sufficient income, adequate food and good nutrition, a healthy environment, parenting, housing and educational early childhood programs all have an effect on young children's well-being, development and health, then on the young school-aged child, and on into the child's development into an adult. — Martha Friendly, early childhood researcher[1]

We know that health is strongly related to the amount of income that people have. But health is also shaped by social determinants of health that are related to income but are important in their own right. Early child development, housing and food security are three strong SDoH. Without doubt, the quality of these three SDoH is significantly influenced by amount of income, but they are also affected by things like family benefits, affordable high-quality early child education and care, regulated rents, affordable/social housing, and public policies that affect the affordability and quality of food.[2]

These three SDoH, which are fundamental to health, are directly shaped by public policy. Establishing the conditions that support a healthy childhood and provide adequate food and housing have been the subject of numerous international human rights agreements — signed by Canadian governments — that require governments to consider these as basic human rights, worthy of universal provision. But a significant proportion of Canadians experience adverse health outcomes associated with Canada lagging well behind other nations in addressing early childhood, housing and food issues. At its worst, many Canadians face the dilemma of whether to "pay the rent or feed the kids." The situation is so bad that Canada is the subject of an ongoing series of rebukes from the United Nations.[3]

EARLY CHILD DEVELOPMENT AND HEALTH

Experiences during the beginnings of the lifespan have both immediate effects — shaping young children's health — and long-lasting effects — providing the foundations for either good or poor health during later periods of the lifespan. These experiences of early childhood produce biological, psychological and social effects that shape health through latency, pathways and cumulative effects.[4]

Most immediately, pregnant women who experience material deprivation and stress are more likely to give birth to children with low birth weights and other health problems. And experiencing deprivation during early childhood is related to a greater incidence of infections, nutritional deficiencies and injuries, as well as asthma.

Early childhood and even pre-birth experiences also have strong latency effects. This means they predispose children to either good or poor health as adults, regardless of later life circumstances.[5] During pregnancy, poor maternal diet, parental risk behaviours and parental stress lead to a greater likelihood that the baby will experience adult-onset diabetes and cardiovascular disease when they grow up. During early childhood, the experience of infections, inadequate diet or adverse housing conditions has immediate and later-in-life health effects. Psychological distress during early life leads to psychological health-related issues in later life, such as lack of a sense of control and self-efficacy.[6]

Children's experience of adverse living conditions may not have immediate health effects, but they can lead to situations that do. These are called pathways effects. An important example of a pathways effect occurs when a young child is not ready to learn upon entering school. By itself, it is not necessarily a health issue, but lack of school readiness — which is strongly related to family income — leads to lower educational and employment attainments. These lower attainments lead to lower-quality and more insecure employment. Difficult employment situations create poor health.[7]

School readiness is therefore both a result of parents' income and educational attainment as well as a predictor of their children's later income and educational attainment. Affordable high-quality early child education is one way of interrupting this sequence. The link between the socio-economic position of parents and their children's developmental outcomes is weak in nations with well-developed early child education programs. A comprehensive early child education program in Canada would be the single best means of improving Canadians' health, a view supported by evidence of the health situations of children and mothers in other developed nations with such programs.[8]

The longer children live under conditions of material and social deprivation, the more likely they are to experience physical and mental health problems later in life. The effects of deprivation have been demonstrated for a variety of chronic diseases, such as heart disease and adult-onset diabetes. The longer children live under deprivation, the more likely they are to develop these afflictions.

THE STATE OF EARLY CHILD DEVELOPMENT

In Canada the state of early child development is cause for concern. The most obvious indicator is the extent to which children are living under conditions of material and social deprivation, i.e., are living in poverty. In 2014, the proportion of children living in poverty in Canada, reported by Campaign 2000, was 19.1 percent. In 2012, the Organization for Economic Cooperation and Development ranked Canada below the OECD average in terms of the child poverty rate, or twenty-second out of thirty-eight wealthy developed nations.[9]

In one international study, Canada ranked last — tied with Ireland — of twenty-five wealthy developed nations in meeting internationally applicable benchmarks for early child-care and education. The report describes these benchmarks as a "set of minimum standards for protecting the rights of children in their most vulnerable and formative years." Canada meets only one of the ten standards. Considering that only 20 percent of Canadian families have access to regulated child-care, these findings are not surprising. Importantly, the report shows that the nations meeting the greatest number of benchmarks have the lowest infant mortality rates and the lowest rates of low birth-weight babies.[10]

FOOD SECURITY AND HEALTH

In Canada, food insecurity is about people — including large numbers of children — going hungry in a relatively rich country that can certainly afford to provide all of its population with the nutrition necessary to lead healthy lives. Food insecurity is about uncertainty — about "the inability to acquire or consume an adequate diet quality or sufficient quantity of food in socially acceptable ways, or the uncertainty that one will be able to do so." Food insecurity is a huge issue in Canada. University of Calgary nutrition professor Lynn McIntyre and Wellesley Institute researcher Laura Anderson state: "A very brief social history of food insecurity in Canada would read simply: Poverty increased, then it deepened. Food insecurity emerged, then it increased in severity."[11]

Whether adults or children, people who suffer from food insecurity are simply not getting as many servings of fruits and vegetables and milk products compared to people in food-secure households. They are getting significantly less minerals and vitamins — falling below the daily requirements for protein, vitamins A and C, thiamine, riboflavin, vitamin B6 and B12, folate, magnesium, phosphorous and zinc; they do not meet current nutrient requirements as outlined by Agriculture Canada. University of Toronto nutrition professor Valerie Tarasuk concludes: "Household food insecurity poses a very real threat to the nutritional status of adults and adolescents."[12]

The dietary deficiencies of food-insecure households contribute to an increased likelihood of chronic diseases as well as difficulties in managing these diseases. Sadly, individuals in food-insecure households are more likely to report the presence of heart disease, diabetes, high blood pressure and food allergies. These greater rates of disease persist even when factors such as age, sex, income adequacy and education are taken into account. In addition, Canadians living with food insecurity are more likely to report poor or fair health as compared to good, very good or excellent health, and to report that they experience poor functional health (pain, hearing and vision

Odds of poor health are 1.5 to 3.5 times higher in food insecure households

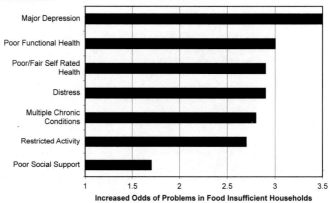

Source: N. Vozoris and V. Tarasuk, "Household Food Insufficiency is Associated with Poorer Health,"
Journal of Nutrition *133: 120–27, 2003.*

problems, restricted mobility), multiple chronic conditions and major depression or distress.[13]

Children living in food-insecure households are more likely to experience a whole range of behavioural, emotional and academic problems than children who are living in households with enough nutritious food. While families appear to be protecting their children from the nutritional effects of food insecurity — mothers often cut back on their own food intake to allow their children to have an adequate diet — "It would appear that they are less successful in protecting their children from the negative psychological impacts of household food insecurity as illustrated by the greater incidence of problems described above."[14]

THE STATE OF FOOD SECURITY

In 2012, Statistics Canada estimated that 12.6 percent of Canadian households were experiencing food insecurity.[15] This figure was even higher for families with children — 15.6 percent. If this kind of finding seems abstract, consider one of the statements that Health Canada used in its measurement of food insecurity: "You and other members of your household worried that food would run out before you got money to buy more."[16] Another tangible indicator of food insecurity has been the appearance and growth of food banks in Canada since the mid-1980s. In March 2015, for instance, 852,137 Canadians made use of food banks — and 36 percent of these "clients" were children: "Food bank use in March was 1.3% higher compared to the same period in 2014 and 26% higher than in 2008, before the start of the global financial crisis."[17]

McIntyre and Anderson note:

> Among children, 16.5 percent lived in households affected by some level of food insecurity, and over 10 percent (nearly 750,000) were in moderately or severely food-insecure homes. Altogether 1.15 million children experienced some level of food insecurity and severe child-level food insecurity was reported at 2.1 percent, affecting 81,600 children.[18]

This survey did not include Aboriginals living on reserves, but McIntyre and Anderson report that 28 percent of Aboriginal households living off-reserve suffered from food insecurity.

Contrary to popular opinion, as disseminated in the news media and in the world of healthy lifestyles promotion, food insecurity is *not* due to lack of basic knowledge, poor budgeting or other personal deficiency. The cause of food insecurity is no secret and is not at all complicated: it is directly related to the level of household income. It is simply a matter of families lacking the financial resources necessary to maintain healthy diets on a daily basis. The families that are most likely to experience food insecurity are the families that are economically deprived and are more likely to be living in areas with few grocery stores — also known as "food deserts."

A 1994 survey showed that lone female-led families were eight times more likely than other families to report their children going hungry, and that trend has not changed in the years since that survey was carried out. When a lone-parent, female-led family receives social assistance, the members became no better off. Those families are thirteen times more likely to report their children going hungry.[19]

The likelihood of hunger among Canadian families increased as a function of a mother reporting fair or poor health (fourfold greater risk), the family being led by a lone parent (threefold greater risk)

We're all paying the price for hunger in Canada

Food insecurity forces people to need emergency rooms, psychiatric hospitals, drug counters and surgery rooms more than others. In Ontario, even moderately food insecure households have health care costs (including medications) that are 49% higher, and extreme food insecure households have health care costs that are 121% higher than food-secure households. The differential between food secure and severe food insecurity is over $1000 per person annually, amounting to almost $1 billion in Ontario alone.

Sources: Z. Feder, 2015, We're All Paying the Price for Hunger in Canada, *Canada Without Poverty* <cwp-csp.ca/2015/08/were-all-paying-the-price-for-hunger-in-canada/; H. Seligman, 2016, "Food Insecurity, Health and Health Care," Centre for Vulnerable Populations, San Francisco General Hospital <cvp.ucsf.edu/resources/Seligman_Issues_Brief_1.24.16.pdf>.

and the family being Aboriginal (60 percent greater risk). Even in Alberta, when the oil economy was booming, conditions were critical. A 2004 Community Health Survey found that 84 percent of Alberta households receiving social assistance were experiencing food insecurity, the highest rate in Canada.[20]

HOUSING AND HEALTH

Friedrich Engels made the link between inadequate housing and adverse health outcomes in 1845 in his book *Condition of the Working Class in England*. Almost a century and a half later, in 1986, the World Health Organization recognized shelter as a prerequisite for health.[21] Indeed, it is an absolute necessity. The evidence indicates that increasing housing insecurity and especially homelessness in Canada are clear threats to health.

According to Toba Bryant, of the University of Ontario Institute

Canada's housing crisis gets international attention

"Everywhere that I visited in Canada, I met people who are homeless and living in inadequate and insecure housing conditions. On this mission I heard of hundreds of people who have died as a direct result of Canada's nation-wide housing crisis. In its most recent periodic review of Canada's compliance with the International Covenant on Economic, Social and Cultural Rights, the United Nations used strong language to label housing and homelessness and inadequate housing as a 'national emergency.' Everything that I witnessed on this mission confirms the deep and devastating impact of this national crisis on the lives of women, youth, children and men."

Source: Miloon Kothari, 2007, "Preliminary Observations of Mission to Canada," United Nations: Special Rapporteur on the Right to Adequate Housing.

of Technology, and Michael Shapcott, of the Wellesley Institute: "The roots of this crisis lie in the federal, provincial, and territorial governments' decisions to cut funding and programs for new social housing and cancel programs over the past three decades, which set the stage for the nation-wide housing crisis and homelessness disaster." The decline in government investment in housing is just another reflection of the weakening the Canadian welfare state and deregulating markets.[22]

The presence of a housing crisis in Canada is particularly noticeable in the increasing numbers of Canadians experiencing housing insecurity and homelessness. Like food insecurity, housing insecurity and homelessness are strongly related to families' and individuals'

Housing need in Canada: Healthy lives start at home

One-third of households in Canada live in substandard conditions or in housing need, as defined by the Canada Mortgage and Housing Corporation, and Canada is the only G8 country without a national housing strategy. In 2013, as many as 1.3 million Canadians had experienced homelessness or extremely insecure housing at some point within the previous five years. There are approximately 15,467 permanent shelter beds in Canada, and in 2009 alone, an average of 14,400 were occupied each night. The number of children staying in shelters increased by more than 50% between 2005 (6,205) and 2009 (9,459). The average length of a shelter stay for families was 50.2 days, more than triple the average stay for the total population of people who experienced homelessness in that same period.

Source: S. Waterston, 2015, Housing Need in Canada: Healthy Lives Start at Home, *Position Statement of the Canadian Paediatric Society <cps.ca/en/documents/position/housing-need>.*

lack of economic resources. Housing insecurity and homelessness are also strongly related to public policy because governments have been reneging on their traditional concerns with meeting the housing and shelter needs of citizens. Despite evidence of the growing housing crisis in Canada, the various levels of government have made only meagre efforts to address this issue. That Canada appears to be sadly failing in meeting its obligations on the housing front is cause for great concern.

WHY HOUSING IS IMPORTANT TO HEALTH

Having shelter from the elements is absolutely essential to a humane existence. Even when shelter is achieved, its quality has profound effects upon health. Housing is tightly connected to health in a number of ways. First, safe, decent housing provides individuals with a quality material environment in which to carry out their lives. Second, good housing provides a platform for self-identity and self-expression. And third, the issue of housing affordability has a serious ripple effect: when people have to spend an excessive amount of their income on housing, they will have less money left over to manage the expenses related to other social determinants of health.[23]

Professor Toba Bryant, of the University of Ontario Institute of Technology, says there are "definitive ... health effects associated with the presence of lead, asbestos, poor heating systems and lack of smoke detectors." Moreover, the "presence of radon, house dust mites, cockroaches, and cold and heat" contribute to health problems. The list of detrimental effects goes on: "environmental tobacco smoke ... dampness and mould, high-rise structures, overcrowding and high density, poor ventilation, and poor housing satisfaction."[24]

A U.K. study explored how heating and dampness influence health. One-quarter of those surveyed said they were unable to afford as much heat as they would have preferred. Another study found that dampness was contributing to the incidence of respiratory illness and making the condition worse. Among children living in homes with damp and mould in Edinburgh, there was an increased risk of wheezing and chesty coughs. Another study saw an increased risk of various symptoms of respiratory illness for both children and adults in damp and mouldy houses as compared to those living in dry dwellings.[25]

But, as health studies professor Toba Bryant points out: "It is difficult to separate the effects of any single variable or sets of variables upon health ... poverty, poor housing, pre-existing illness frequently cluster together." Still, one U.K. study — *Home Sweet Home: The Impact of Poor Housing on Health* — was able to get around this problem. Among more than 13,000 citizens, poor housing conditions during childhood played a significant and independent role in determining health outcomes: the worse the conditions, the greater the likelihood of severe or moderate ill health at age thirty-three. Children who experienced overcrowded housing conditions up to age eleven had a higher likelihood of infectious disease as adults. In adulthood, conditions of overcrowding increased the likelihood of respiratory disease. The experience of living in poor housing in either the past or the present contributed to the likelihood of poor health. The worst situation was to have lived in adverse housing in the past and to be still living in poor housing in the present. Adverse housing conditions during childhood can also predict early death: associations were found between the lack of a private indoor tapped water supply and increased mortality from coronary heart disease, and between poor ventilation and overall mortality.[26]

The most drastic housing connection to health is homelessness. Homeless people are much more likely to experience numerous physical and mental health problems than the members of the general population. Homeless people experience very high levels of respiratory disease, alcohol and drug dependence, and mental health problems, and they are prone to suicide, accidents and violence. A Toronto survey identified the profound health problems associated with not having shelter. It found that homeless people were at a much higher risk than the general population for chronic respiratory diseases, arthritis or rheumatism, hypertension, asthma, epilepsy and diabetes.[27]

Homeless people also die at a younger age than do people in the general population. Between 1979 and 1990, 71 percent of homeless people in Toronto who died were younger than 70 years old. Regarding deaths in the general population, the proportion below age 70 was 38 percent. Dr. Stephen Hwang, of St. Michael's Hospital in Toronto, found that men who used shelters in were eight times more likely to die than were men in the general population. Still another study found that among homeless people in Toronto, death rates were a very high 515 per 100,000 person-years for homeless women aged 18–44 years and 438 per 100,000 person-years for homeless women aged 45–64 years. The likelihood of an early death was ten times greater for younger homeless women than for women in the general population.[28]

THE STATE OF HOUSING

Affordable housing is that which costs less than 30 percent of before-tax household income. If the cost of housing is over that percentage, people are considered to have "core housing need." On that count, a significant proportion of Canadian households experience difficulty affording housing, and the numbers have been increasing since 1991. This situation is especially the case for Canadian renters, who tend to have low levels of income and wealth.[29]

Renters, women, immigrants and Indigenous people experience housing insecurity

Housing insecure/core housing need groups:

- Renters, at 26.4 percent compared to owners at 6.5 percent
- Female lone-parent households and female single-person households
- Off-reserve Indigenous renters (34.7%)
- Immigrant households (29.6%)
- Senior renters (28.9%)
- Indigenous lone-parent households had the highest incidence (51.8%)
- Non-Indigenous lone-parent households had an incidence of 40.6 percent.

Note: Percentages are from 2011 data.
Source: T. Bryant and M. Shapcott, 2016, "Housing," in D. Raphael (ed.), Social Determinants of Health: Canadian Perspectives, third edition, Canadian Scholars' Press.

The proportion of tenants in Canadian cities spending more than 30 percent of their income on rent is high (43 percent in Vancouver, 42 percent in Toronto and 36 percent in Montreal). And the proportion spending more than 50 percent — putting them at risk of imminent homelessness — is also strikingly high (22 percent in Vancouver, 20 percent in Toronto and 18 percent in Montreal). Rental costs have far outpaced income increases among low-income renters in virtually all Canadian urban areas (for Vancouver the discrepancy is 45 percent; for Toronto, 62 percent; Montreal data is not available).[30]

QUALITY EARLY CHILD DEVELOPMENT, FOOD AND HOUSING EQUAL BETTER HEALTH

The situation concerning early child development, food security and housing in Canada is disturbing — and we have every reason to believe that the situation has only worsened since the onset of the 2008 recession.

In 1998 the Toronto Disaster Relief Committee declared

The one percent solution

In 1998 the Toronto Disaster Relief Committee launched a national campaign called the "One Percent Solution." The campaign grew out of an observation by Dr. David Hulchanski, a leading Canadian housing scholar, who noted that in the mid 1990s all governments together spent about 1 percent of their overall budgets on housing. Doubling that amount — or adding an additional 1 percent — would fund a comprehensive, national housing strategy, with these key elements:

- supply (increase the number of rental units)
- affordability (ensure the new units are affordable to the households that need the new housing the most)
- supports (programs for those who require special services)
- rehabilitation (funding to maintain housing to a proper standard)
- emergency relief (special support for people who are already homeless)

In 2008, that would amount to $2 billion added to the $2 billion spent. The Federation of Canadian Municipalities called for a similar response, setting their target at $3.35 billion.

Sources: The Toronto Disaster Relief Committee, 1998, The One Percent Solution; M. Shapcott, 2009, "Housing," in D. Raphael (ed.), Social Determinants of Health: Canadian Perspectives, second edition, Canadian Scholars' Press.

homelessness a national disaster. Considering the situation of children in Canada and the crisis of food and housing insecurity, additional calls to direct attention to the situation of children, food and housing insecurity would be timely. Canada is a signatory to numerous United Nations covenants and agreements that call attention to meeting the basic needs of its citizens, but all the evidence indicates that Canada is failing to meet its obligations under these agreements.

SOCIAL EXCLUSION

Social exclusion ... broadly describes both the structures and the dynamic processes of inequality among groups in society, which, over time, structure access to critical resources that determine the quality of membership in society and ultimately produce and reproduce a complex of unequal outcomes. — Grace-Edward Galabuzi, political scientist[1]

In Canada, the people who are most vulnerable to material and social disadvantage — those with low incomes and little wealth — are more likely to be Indigenous people, people of colour, recent immigrants, women and/or people with disabilities. They are also the Canadians more likely to experience the adverse health outcomes associated with the inequitable distribution of society's resources. Moreover, these Canadians have little power to force governments and policy-makers to address these issues. People in this situation are experiencing social exclusion.

SOCIAL EXCLUSION HAS FOUR ASPECTS

Paul White, of the University of Sheffield, identifies four aspects of social exclusion. The first is a denial of participation in civic affairs as a result of legal sanctions or other institutional mechanisms. This occurs, for example, when laws and regulations prevent non-status residents or migrants from participating in a variety of societal activities. It may also result from systemic forms of discrimination based on race, gender, ethnicity or disability status, among other factors. For example, many new Canadians are not able to practise their professions due to myriad regulations and procedures. While Ontario garners more than 50 percent of immigrants to Canada, including a large number of physicians who were licensed in their homeland, at the end of the 1990s, only twenty-four residency positions were available to internationally trained physicians. If there were a large number of graduates from local medical schools, they received the spots, not the new Canadians. Towards the end of the 2000s, the number had improved to two hundred spots a year, but there were still many more applicants than spots available.

The second form of social exclusion is the denial of social goods, such as health care, education, housing, income security and language services, and the lack of a means of reducing discrimination. Some marginalized groups — Indigenous Canadians, people of colour, recent immigrants, women and people with disabilities — have lower incomes than Canadians of European descent. They are more likely to be unable to afford housing and to find it more difficult to get access to necessary medical services.

The third type is exclusion from social production, which involves a denial of the opportunity to participate in and contribute to social activities, such as clubs, recreational activities and cultural events. Much of this deprivation has to do with their lack of financial resources.

Economic exclusion is the fourth type, and it occurs in cases where individuals cannot get access to economic resources and opportunities, such as participation in paid work. For example, evidence shows systemic differences in levels of employment, employment security and training opportunities between non-disabled Canadians of European descent and members of these other groups. Social exclusion is both a social determinant of health in itself and also has a huge impact on many other social determinants of health.[2]

INDIGENOUS PEOPLES AND HEALTH

Janet Smylie and Michelle Firestone, of the Centre for Research in Inner City Health in Toronto, show how the health of Indigenous peoples in Canada — First Nations, Dene, Métis and Inuit — is inextricably tied up with their history of colonization. In Canada this history has taken the form of legislation such as the Indian Act of 1876, disregard for the land claims of Métis peoples, relocation of Inuit communities and the establishment of residential schools, as well as not honouring signed treaties. Through colonization, Indigenous peoples were dislocated from their lands, which undermined their economies and livelihoods. The result has been their systemic disadvantage in terms of the social determinants of health and the resulting adverse health outcomes.

In 2011, Indigenous people numbered 1.4 million and constituted about 4.3 percent of the population in Canada. There are numerous gaps in the social determinants of health between Indigenous people and non-Indigenous Canadians. Smylie and Firestone point out that, in 2011, the average income of Indigenous men was $33,570 and of women was $26,341, which represented 68 percent of the average income of non-Indigenous men and 79 percent of the average income of non-Indigenous women. The situation was worse for Indigenous

Colonizing Indigenous peoples in Canada

The Indian Act

"The first Indian Act of 1876 reflects governmental policies of assimilation of Aboriginal populations in Canada and appropriation of Aboriginal lands.... The Constitution Act of 1867 and subsequent Indian Acts legalized the removal of First Nations communities, which had signed treaties, from their homelands to 'reserve lands' that were controlled by the Government of Canada on behalf of 'Indians.' The Indian Acts of 1876, 1880, and 1884 later outlawed First Nations ceremonies such as the sundance and potlatch and gave the Indian agent authority over the foods, goods, and travel available to on-reserve First Nations peoples. These policies also supported the abduction of Aboriginal children to residential schools, where language and culture were actively suppressed."

Disregard of Métis Land Claims

"In 1869, the Hudson Bay Company transferred its lands in Canada's Northwest and authority for these lands to the Government of Canada.... At the time of the transfer, First Nations and Métis were by far the biggest populations living in these areas.... This transfer did not include any provision for the First Nations and Métis peoples who were living on these lands, and social unrest was therefore a predictable outcome.... The disruption of Métis families and communities resulting from federal governmental disregard for and appropriation of their lands has had a long-standing impact on Métis.... Prior to the Hudson Bay land transfer in Manitoba and the uprising in Batoche, many Métis families on the Prairies were economically prospering. Following these events, Métis struggled economically and commonly faced racial prejudice from European settlers, which, in turn, limited job prospects."

Relocation of Inuit Communities

"During and after the Second World War, the federal government had a policy of 'encouraging' Inuit to relocate into permanent villages in areas selected by the government.... One of the first relocation attempts occurred in 1934. Twenty-two Inuit from Kinngait (Cape Dorset), 18 from Mittimatalk/Tununiq (Pond Inlet), and 12 from Pangnirtuuq (Pangnirtung) were transported to Dundas Harbour. During the 1950s and 1960s, many more Inuit families were moved from their traditional lands to permanent settlements. The hunting conditions of the new sites were usually suboptimal, interfering with traditional food supply. In addition to food insecurity, unemployment, and housing issues, the move to permanent settlements was accompanied by outbreaks of tuberculosis. By 1964, more than 70 percent of Keewatin Inuit had been in TB sanatoria."

Source: J. Smylie, 2009, "The Health of Aboriginal People," in D. Raphael (ed.), Social Determinants of Health: Canadian Perspectives, *second edition, Canadian Scholars' Press.*

people living on reserves. Their incomes as a percentage of non-Indigenous incomes were, for men, 40 percent, and for women, 61 percent. Even Indigenous people living off-reserve had incomes that were well below the incomes of non-Indigenous Canadians. Similarly, in 2011, 25 percent of Indigenous households had incomes below the low-income cut-offs (Canada's unofficial poverty line), in contrast to 15 percent of households that were not Indigenous.[3]

In 2009, the overall Indigenous unemployment rate was 14 percent in Canada, compared to 8 percent of non-Indigenous households.[4] For First Nations people living on-reserve the figure was 23 percent, which was almost twice the rate (12.3 percent) of First Nations living off-reserve. Education levels also differ widely between Indigenous and non-Indigenous Canadians. The 2012 Aboriginal Peoples Survey found that 72 percent of First Nations people living off-reserve, 42 percent of Inuit and 77 percent of Métis aged 18 to 44 had a high school diploma or equivalent. But that figure was only 56 percent for Indigenous people on-reserve, and only 24 percent of First Nations on-reserve were post-secondary graduates, as compared to 40 percent of the general Canadian population.

**Socio-economic gaps between Indigenous and
non-Indigenous people are persistent**

	1981	1991	2001	2006
Bachelor degree and above (%)				
Indigenous	3.4	6.2	9.0	11.4
Non-Indigenous	14.3	17.0	26.5	29.0
Gap	10.9	10.8	17.5	17.6
Unemployment rate (%)				
Indigenous	14.8	21.7	17.1	13.3
Non-Indigenous	7.3	11.5	7.6	6.7
Gap	7.4	10.2	9.5	6.6
Median individual income ($)				
Indigenous	7,666	14,448	16,391	19,507
Non-Indigenous	12,712	20,872	23,912	25,644
Gap (%)	60.3	69.4	68.5	76.1

Source: F. Mitrou et al., 2014, "Gaps in Indigenous Disadvantage Not Closing: A Census Cohort Study of Social Determinants of Health in Australia, Canada, and New Zealand from 1981–2006," bmc Public Health 14.

The level of food insecurity among Indigenous people is strikingly high. Of those living off-reserve, 21 percent experience food insecurity and 8.4 percent reported severe food insecurity. Among those living on-reserve, more than half of households are moderately to severely food insecure. Among the Inuit population, 34 percent of homes with three- to five-year-old children were food insecure and had to skip meals, with 24 percent reporting severe child food insecurity.

Indigenous people in Canada are also four times more likely to be living in crowded housing. Some 38 percent of Inuit in Innuit Nunatt (northern Inuit territories) live in crowded housing, as compared to 11 percent of Indigenous people and 3 percent of the non-Indigenous population.

The life expectancy of Indigenous people is five to fourteen years less than that of the Canadian population, with Inuit men and women showing the shortest lives. Among Indigenous people, infant mortality rates — children dying before their first year — are one and a half to four times greater than the overall Canadian rate.

The rates of infectious and chronic diseases are also much higher in the Indigenous population in Canada. Suicide rates are five to six times higher than in the non-Indigenous population. "Diabetes is of particular concern … the proportion of the population reporting a diagnosis of diabetes was highest for First Nations individuals living on reserve and aged 18 years and older (15.3 percent), followed by First Nations individuals living off reserve and aged 12 years and older (8.7 percent)." Indigenous peoples have high rates of major depression, problems with alcohol and experience of sexual abuse during childhood.

Rates of infectious diseases are higher for tuberculosis, pertussis, rubella, shigellosis and chlamydia, and Indigenous children are more likely to be hospitalized or to die from respiratory illness. Indigenous people make up 12.2 percent of new HIV infections and 8.9 percent of those living with HIV in Canada. Finally, the tuberculosis rate among Indigenous people in Canada is more than five times the rate for the Canadian population as a whole and it comprised 23 percent of reported TB cases in 2012. All of these afflictions are related to the effects of poverty.[5]

NEW CANADIANS AND PEOPLE OF COLOUR AND HEALTH

Immigration during the first decade of the twenty-first century accounted for more than half of the increase in the Canadian population and 70 percent of the increase in the number of people in the workplace. By the end of the second decade, immigration will account for all of the net growth in the labour force. Since the 1960s, over three-quarters of the immigrants to Canada have come from the Global South. The majority of them are "racialized" immigrants (once called "visible minorities"). One-third of the members of racialized groups in Canada are Canadian-born; the other two-thirds are immigrants.[6]

Members of racialized groups in Canada experience a whole range of difficult living circumstances that undermine their general well-being and health. The problematic income situation of new Canadians is common across virtually all immigrant groups to Canada and is most apparent in terms of poverty rates. The overall poverty rate is only 6 percent for non-racialized Canadians, yet it is close to 20 percent for racialized Canadians, almost four times higher. The average income for all racialized groups tends to be well below that of Canadian earners in general, and in some cases the gap is more than $10,000. From 2000 to 2005, incomes increased for non-racialized Canadians but declined for racialized Canadians. Unemployment rates are higher (8.6 percent for racialized workers versus 6.2 for workers who are not racialized).

New immigrants of colour show particularly pronounced levels of poverty. One study looked at changes in the Toronto Census Metropolitan areas from 1971 to 2000 of these poverty rates. In 1971, the average income of racialized women was close to that of women of European descent. Indeed, the incomes of South and West Asian women were higher than those of the European-descent average. But over the period from 1970 to 2000, the average income of racialized women declined relative to women of European descent, and now their average incomes are at 70 to 80 percent of the European-descent group.[7]

For men, the figures are equally dramatic. In 1970, the incomes of men in racialized groups were already falling behind the incomes of

Racialized people earn less in Canada

The employment earnings for racialized workers are lower than non-racialized workers—except for the small number of Canadians who identify as Japanese:

- Koreans: They earn 69 cents for every dollar a non-racialized worker earns, with an annual earnings gap of $11,403.
- Latin Americans: They earn 70 cents for every dollar a non-racialized worker earns, with an earnings gap of $11,091.
- West Asians: They earn 70 cents for every dollar a non-racialized worker earns, with an earnings gap of $11,053.
- Blacks: They earn 75.6 cents for every dollar a non-racialized worker earns, with an earnings gap of $9,101.
- South East Asians: They earn 77.5 cents for every dollar a non-racialized worker earns, with an earnings gap of $8,395.

Source: S. Block and G.E. Galabuzi, 2011, Colour Coded Labour Markets: The Gap for Racialized Worker, CCPA/Wellesley Institute.

men of European descent, averaging about 75 to 85 percent of their levels. The one exception was Asian and West Asian men, whose incomes were 10 percent higher than those of men of European descent. But by 2000, the average incomes of Asian and West Asian men had declined to 75 percent of European-descent men. The incomes of the rest of the racialized men had gone down to 60 to 75 percent of the incomes of men of European descent.

While the average poverty rates for people of European descent were slightly over 10 percent, the poverty rates for other groups were

Racialized people are more likely to have low incomes

	Men	Women	Total
Arab	32.0	33.1	32.5
Black	22.3	25.5	24.0
Chinese	19.6	19.4	19.5
Filipino	8.0	8.3	8.2
Latin American	19.8	21.3	20.6
Japanese	8.5	10.1	9.4
Korean	38.1	38.2	38.2
South Asian	16.1	16.3	16.4
Southeast Asian	17.7	19.1	18.5
West Asian	31.5	33.4	32.4
Multiple visible	14.0	14.6	14.3
Total racialized	19.4	20.1	19.8
Total non-racialized	5.9	6.9	6.4

Source: G.E. Galabuzi, 2016, "Social Exclusion," in D. Raphael (ed.), Social Determinants of Health: Canadian Perspectives, third edition, Table 17.3, p. 396, Canadian Scholars' Press [data source: Census 2006].

strikingly high: Indigenous people (20 percent), Arab and West Asian (30 percent), South Asian (20 percent), East Asian (20 percent), African (39 percent), Caribbean (22 percent) and South and Central American (20 percent).[8]

In the past, with the exception of Indigenous peoples, there tended not to be significant health differences between racialized groups in Canada. Much of this was probably due to the "healthy immigrant effect," whereby immigrants — many of them persons of colour

Anxiety over immigration rules and the cost of immigration bad for newcomer health

In the last decade, immigration and citizenship acts in Canada have been changed numerous times. All the changes leave many immigrants and refugees unsure of their status in Canada and the procedures they need to go through to become citizens. As one said, "Not being a citizen is very unsettling. What if the government changes its rules again, turning the citizenship requirement to 10, 15 years instead of four?" This anxiety, coupled with the often onerous "transportation loans," fills immigrant lives with stress and fear. Such stress often reignites traumas from the past, all of which can lead to mental health issues for newcomers. *Example*: Because of the IFH cuts, a Congolese pastor who was imprisoned for his political opinions is not able to receive therapy. While in jail he was whipped and beaten, and he now exhibits signs of post-traumatic stress disorder (PTSD) and high anxiety. He fears for the family members he was forced to leave behind when he fled the country.

Sources: A. Ahmed, S. Denetto and N. DePape, 2015, "Deepening the Divide," in L. Fernandez, S. MacKinnon and J. Silver, The Social Determinants of Health in Manitoba, CCPA-Manitoba; Canadian Council for Refugees, Interim Federal Health Program: Impacts of the Cuts <ccrweb. ca/en/ifh>.

— showed superior health status to non-Indigenous people born in Canada. However, by 2005, the health of non-European immigrants had deteriorated compared to Canadian-born non-Indigenous residents and European immigrants. Recent non-European immigrants (less than ten years in Canada) became twice as likely to report deterioration in health. Long-term non-European immigrants were also more likely to report ill health, though recent and long-term European immigrants did not. As well, non-European immigrants were 50 percent more likely to be frequent visitors to doctors than was the Canadian-born population.[9]

A number of social determinants of health are related to this trend of declining health among racialized immigrants, including low incomes, lower levels of education and a lack of support from others. Studies indicate that recent immigrants of colour are experiencing greater incidences of mental health problems and housing and food insecurity than are Canadians of European descent. The pattern of increasing economic and racial concentration in Canadian urban areas is another cause for concern. In the United States, a concentration of economically disadvantaged racialized groups has been associated with adverse health outcomes.[10]

WOMEN AND HEALTH

Women are particularly subject to social determinants that have a negative effect on their health. Much of this has to do with the responsibility that women traditionally have for raising children and caring for the health needs of families. Women are less likely to be working full-time and less likely to be eligible for unemployment benefits. Women are more likely to be employed in lower paying occupations and more likely to experience discrimination in the workplace. In addition, the public policy decisions associated with economic and social security — such as the failure to raise minimum wages and social assistance benefits, the reduction of access to public health services, limitations on the availability of affordable housing and of government-supported, quality child-care, and the introduction of restrictive workfare requirements — disproportionately hurt women more than men.[11]

Women earn less than men do, regardless of occupation. In 2015, Canadian women's hourly pay was about 84 percent of men's pay. The gap has disappeared in Prince Edward Island but remains a significant 20% in Alberta and Newfoundland and Labrador and close to 10 percent or more elsewhere. Even accounting for factors such as work experience and job-related responsibilities, gender differences remain in wages between men and women. Statistics Canada stated:

Women still earn significantly less than men, even in 2015

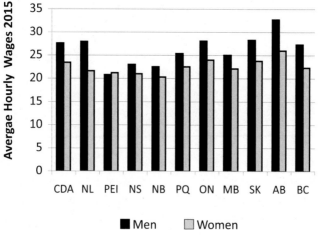

Source: Statistics Canada, 2015, Labour-force survey estimates (LFS), wages of employees, Table 282-0073.

"Despite the long list of productivity-related factors, a substantial portion of the gender gap cannot be explained by traditional measures of education and experience."[12] Indeed, Ann Curry-Stevens points out:

> Despite popular opinion that women have achieved equality with men, women's incomes remain … lower than men.…
> At first glance, one might think that this is a function of choice and that women might work fewer hours to accumulate this income. But when we compare income levels of women who work full-time to those of men who work full-time, the earnings remain inequitable.[13]

In addition, since women work fewer hours than men, their total income is much less. A predominant reason for why women work fewer hours than men is the lack of affordable and quality child-care and the fact that women are usually responsible for dealing with the burden of reconciling work and family. The problem of balancing employment and family contributes to family stress in general and to women's stress in particular. Affordable, high-quality child-care is an important means not only of enabling women to participate in the employment workplace as equals to men but also of promoting women's health and well-being.

Women do seem to have a health advantage when it comes to outliving men. Canadian women have a life expectancy of 81.3 years compared to 78.1 for men. But the higher mortality rate and lower life expectancy of men have been misinterpreted to mean that women enjoy superior health. This interpretation completely ignores the higher prevalence of chronic conditions in women, particularly in later life. Moreover, women's life expectancy rates appear to be converging with those of men in industrialized countries, mostly due to improvements in men's life expectancy. Just as women's life expectancy increased dramatically in the middle of the twentieth century as a result of reductions in maternal mortality, the current pattern of life expectancy observed between women and men may not hold in the future.[14]

PEOPLE WITH DISABILITIES AND HEALTH

Too often disability is seen in medical rather than in social terms. While disability is clearly related to physical and mental functions, the primary issue is whether society is willing to provide the supports and opportunities that are necessary if people with physical and mental challenges are to participate fully in Canadian life. People with disabilities are people attempting to live — as are all Canadians — fulfilling lives. Instead they are frequently seen as a collection of challenges. Indeed, the problems that people with disabilities experience have more to do with society's response to their disabilities than with the disabilities themselves.

Canada's public policy responses to the challenges that people with disabilities face generally lag behind those of other wealthy developed nations. People with disabilities are less likely to be employed. In 2011, only 47 percent of Canadians with disabilities aged 15–64 were in the labour force, compared to 74 percent of their non-disabled contemporaries. When they are employed, they earn less than people without disabilities. In 2011, the average salary of the employed people with disabilities was $20,420, compared with $31,160 for those without disabilities.[15]

Those who are not in the workforce are usually forced to rely upon social assistance benefits, which are very low in Canada. In most cities the payments do not bring individuals even close to the poverty line. Canada is one of the most frugal countries (twenty-eighth out

Women's health is influenced by violence — direct injury and by stress from fear of violence against themselves or their children by men

*Women victims of spousal violence are more than **twice as likely** to be injured as are male victims (42% vs 18%).*

*Women are **3 times** more likely to:*
• report chronic violence — 11 or more incidents of violence (20% vs 7%).
• be sexually assaulted, beaten, choked or threatened with a gun (35% vs 10%).

*Women were almost **7 times** more likely to fear for their lives (33% vs 5%).*

Over one-half of Canadian women have experienced at least one incident of physical or sexual violence since the age of 16.

51%

• 40,000 arrests from domestic violence
• 12% of violent crime
• Only 22% of incidents are reported

Sources: Canadian Women's Foundation, 2015, Moving Women out of Violence: Fact Sheet, May <canadianwomen.org/sites/canadianwomen.org/files/FactSheet-StopViolence-ACTIVE - May2015. pdf>; Tina Hotton Mahony, 2011, Women and the Criminal Justice System, Statistics Canada <statcan.gc.ca/pub/89-503-x/2010001/article/11416-eng.pdf>; Statistics Canada, 1993, "The Violence against Women Survey," The Daily, November 18.

of thirty-four OECD nations) in its allocation of benefits and supports to people with disabilities.[16]

The Canadian Council on Social Development reports that much of the distress has to do with the workplace being either unable or unwilling to accommodate the needs of persons with disabilities: "Among unemployed persons with disabilities, 56% say they require some type of work aid or job modification, with job redesign (required by 42%) and modified work hours (35%) being the most commonly cited." Ironically, as the Council points out, many of the required modifications are rather minor. The Council' report quoted the Alberta Abilities Foundation:

> While the requirement for workplace accommodations is fairly high, these accommodations are usually not terribly costly.... [The] annual workplace accommodation costs are under $1,500 for almost all workers who have a disability... for just over half of those requiring some type of accommodation, the estimated cost would be less than $500 per person per year; for one-third, the cost would be $500 to $1,500 per year; and for 16%, the cost was estimated at over $1,500. These costs are probably much lower than many employers realize. For many persons with disabilities, an employer's reluctance to provide accommodation on the job can be extremely disheartening and frustrating: "Employers are still ignorant about what it takes to hire and accommodate a person with a disability."[17]

SOCIAL INCLUSION EQUALS BETTER HEALTH

Through social exclusion, certain groups of people are denied the opportunity to participate in civic society. They are denied an acceptable standard of living, meaning they are essentially unable to contribute to society. All of these elements occur in tandem with the experience of material and social deprivation associated with the social determinants of health. These experiences have strong effects upon health.

Social exclusion happens to people as a result of government policy and the socio-economic structures of racism, sexism and ableism, not as a result of the characteristics of individuals. What all of these groups share is a relative lack of power in society and the inability to influence public policy. Changing this lack of socio-political power will do as much for the health of Canadians as all the medical research and health care improvements that occupy so much public debate and political activity.

PUBLIC POLICY AND THE SOCIAL DETERMINANTS OF HEALTH

Policies shape how money, power and material resources flow through society and therefore affect the determinants of health. Advocating healthy public policies is the most important strategy we can use to act on the determinants of health. — Canadian Public Health Association[1]

In 2008, the World Health Organization's Commission on Social Determinants of Health noted that the "unequal distribution of health-damaging experiences is not in any sense a 'natural' phenomenon." Rather, it stated, these conditions are "the result of a toxic combination of poor social policies and programmes, unfair economic arrangements, and bad politics."[2]

Experiences in Canada and abroad show that governments and policy-makers can shape public policies to support and encourage health. In fact, governments have a responsibility to do something to improve the health of their citizens. The policies that can achieve this goal are well documented and have been put into effective practice in many nations. These policies result in better quality and more equitable distribution of the social determinants of health.[3]

As stated previously, Canada falls well behind other nations in implementing such public policies. We need to consider the economic, political and ideological forces that prevent actions to improve the health of the populace from being taken. One of the problems is that within the political economy of Canada — that is, the operation of the country's political and economic systems — the market, rather than the government through its laws and regulations, is the dominant institution shaping the SDoH. The government policy-making associated with this political economy generally does not place a priority on the SDoH. To overcome the problem of ill health among Canadians, we must find a more reasonable balance between the market (and those groups that control it) and the groups in Canadian society whose voices have less influence upon governments and policy-makers.

THE CONTEXT FOR PUBLIC POLICY

Public policy is defined as a course of action or inaction taken by public authorities — usually governments — to address a given problem or set of problems. These activities are first of all anchored in the values and beliefs that shape whether a situation will even be perceived as being a public — rather than an individual — problem. If the problem is perceived to be a public concern, the next step is for the government to respond appropriately to address the issue.

There are numerous issues that may or may not be seen as public problems worthy of public policy solutions. Take child-care, for example. The importance of families having access to regulated, high-quality and affordable child-care is well documented. High-quality child-care supports child development, allows women to enter the workforce on equal terms with men, reduces poverty rates and provides many other benefits to the society as a whole.[4]

Even so, in Canada, the lack of high-quality, affordable childcare — outside of Quebec — has not been perceived by elected representatives and policy-makers as a public problem worthy of a public policy solution. This not the case in the Nordic countries and in many continental European nations, where public policy is influenced by values of promoting child well-being, gender equity and societal cohesion.[5]

The role that values play in influencing public policy is also starkly apparent when we consider issues of employment security and working conditions, wages and benefits, and food and housing security. Most European nations have labour legislation and regulations that provide employment security and require benefits and retraining opportunities be provided to both full-time and part-time workers. National commissions ensure that levels of wages and benefits allow citizens to avoid material and social deprivation and housing and food insecurity. These nations implement public policies that provide citizens with the living and working conditions necessary for health. Because of this, these policies also ensure the well-being of the entire society. The primary values shaping such public policies are, in the case of the social democratic Nordic nations, the promotion of equality and, in the case of the conservative continental European nations, the maintaining of social solidarity.[6]

The role of values is also especially relevant when we consider the issue of poverty rates. In many nations, reducing poverty and promoting early child development are central concerns of governments and policy-makers at all levels. These nations also make a commitment to reduce the impacts upon health of risks that may arise during the lifecourse (i.e., adverse living conditions, unemployment, disability and illness, and loss of income upon retirement). These approaches are far less common in Canada.

Public policy is therefore especially important for improving the quality and distribution of the social determinants of health by setting employment standards, wage levels and the nature and quality of benefits, and by determining whether these benefits are universal or targeted. Among other actions, governments can also improve the quality and distribution of the SDoH through housing and child-care policies, supporting retraining programs and providing educational opportunities.

As one example, making sure everyone has an adequate income would impact a variety of the SDoH. Promoting a more equitable distribution of income would respond to issues of housing and food insecurity, early child development and social exclusion. Policies focused on increasing employment security and improving working conditions would likewise make a positive contribution to distributing income, reducing housing and food insecurity, fostering early child development and reducing social exclusion.

A common theme in such public policies is assisting Canadians with managing risk across the lifecourse. University of Bristol researcher Mary Shaw and her colleagues identify the significant lifecourse transitions during which anyone can be vulnerable if they experience disadvantage. These include foetal development, nutritional growth and health in childhood, leaving home, entering the labour market and retirement, among others. Material disadvantage and the absence of societal supports during these key periods work against health. The link between the navigation of these transitions and the impact of the social determinants of health is striking. For example, proper foetal development, nutritional growth and health in childhood are clearly linked to income, food and housing; entering the labour market, job loss or insecurity are linked to employment security and working conditions; and episodes of illness are linked with the quality of the social safety net.

There are two types of health risks: universal risks, such as the life transitions identified by Shaw and her colleagues; and non-universal risks, such as premature disease, injuries and accidents, and family breakups, among others. Societies individualize all of these risks when they do not provide public, collectively organized responses to these situations, such as the universal provision of benefits and services. Collective approaches to managing risk are essential for meeting the needs of the majority of Canadians.[7]

In particular, as Professor Gosta Esping-Andersen points out, managing risk during childhood is essential. The primary factors shaping children's cognitive abilities are health, income security and developmental priming mechanisms that set the stage for lifelong learning. Of foremost importance for achieving health and minimizing poverty is, he maintains, the establishment of a strong welfare state that provides security to its citizens — and it is here where Canada appears to be sorely lagging. Esping-Andersen's analysis is consistent with the social determinants of health concept. When it comes to the developmental priming mechanisms, he sees the provision of universal high-quality child-care as essential. The limited extent to which Canada is meeting these requirements is discouraging.[8]

POPULATION HEALTH AND PUBLIC POLICY

Canada is among the wealthiest nations in the world. In 2014, Canada's per capita GDP was US$44,057, placing us twelfth among thirty-four OECD nations.[9] Given this relatively wealthy position, how do Canada's health indicators compare to other nations?

Canada's ranking in life expectancy is midrange and has been consistently falling since the early 1990s. The current ranking is thirteenth of thirty-four nations for men and seventeenth for women. The recent history of the country's infant mortality rate, which is often identified as the most sensitive indicator of overall population health, is also telling. In 1980, Canada's infant mortality rate was 10 deaths per 1000 births, which gave it a relative ranking of tenth out of thirty-four OECD nations. By 2005, Canada had improved that to 5.3/1000, a significant achievement, but that decline failed to match the pattern in other OECD nations — so much so that Canada's ranking over that period fell from tenth to twenty-fourth. The infant mortality

For such a wealthy nation, Canada is not doing so good on health

Health indicator	Canada's score	Canada's ranking (1=best)
Life expectancy — total	81.5 years	13th of 34
Life expectancy — males	77.8 years	13th of 34
Life expectancy — females	82.6 years	17th of 34
Premature years of life lost prior to age 70 — males	3675/100,000	6th of 34
Premature years of life lost prior to age 70 — females	2332/100,000	16th of 34
Deaths from ischemic heart disease	95/100,000	17th of 34
Deaths from cerebrovascular disease	38/100,000	2nd of 34
Deaths from cancer	207/100,000	22th of 34
Deaths from cancer — males	249/100,000	10th of 34
Deaths from cancer — females	178/100,000	27th of 34
Infant mortality	4.8/1000	27th of 34
Low birth-weight rates	6.1/100	14th of 34

Source: Organisation for Economic Cooperation and Development (OECD), 2015, Health at a Glance.

rate is now 4.8/1000, an improvement in absolute terms, but now our rank is a dismal twenty-seventh.[10]

Most of the nations doing better than Canada in both infant mortality and low birth-weight rates are not as wealthy as Canada in terms of per capita GDP. For example, the Finnish economy produces US$4,000 per capita less than the Canadian, yet Finland's rates for infant mortality and low birth weights are far lower than Canada's.

MATERIAL AND SOCIAL SECURITY

The level of citizens' material and social security is an important determinant of well-being, and a country's commitment to this is indicated in total public expenditure on its provision. The best measure of this is the extent to which a nation collects revenues and transfers them to citizens in the form of benefits, programs and services, such as education, employment training, social assistance, family supports, pensions, health and social services, and housing. In 2014, Canada allocated 17 percent of its GDP on such spending — which placed Canada twenty-sixth on a list of thirty-four OECD countries. Nations such as France, Finland, Belgium and Denmark all allocate over 30 percent of their GDP on such public expenditures. The United States allocated 19.2 percent of its GDP towards these expenditures, also above Canada.[11]

How exactly do these social expenditures play out in Canada? Not very well. Canada ranks thirtieth on spending on families, twentieth on active labour policy, thirtieth on pensions and thirty-first in disability. Clearly, Canada does little to assure economic and social security for children in families, workers requiring retraining, seniors living on pensions and people living with a disability.

Canada ranks very low among industrialized countries on public social expenditure

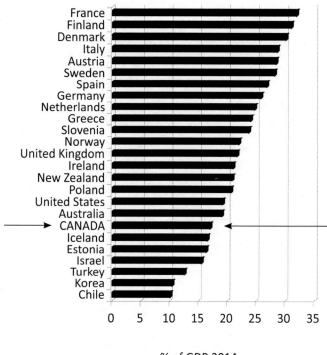

% of GDP 2014

Source: OECD, 2014, Social Policy and Data, Social Expenditure Database <stats.OECD.org/Index. aspx?datasetcode=SOCX_AGG>.

Canada ranks close to last among industrialized countries on public expenditures on families

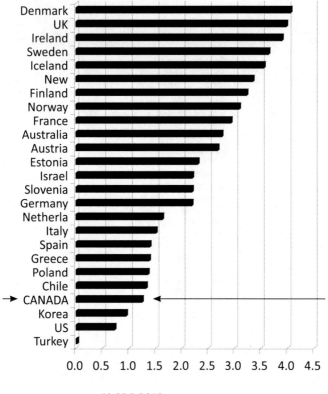

% GDP 2012

Source: OECD, 2016, Social Expenditure Database (SOCX) <OECD.org/social/expenditure.htm>.

INCOME AND INCOME DISTRIBUTION

Interestingly, nations that spend less for social security are also the ones with less income equality. A high degree of income inequality in a country has much to do with government reluctance to implement policies that redistribute income and wealth, thus leaving it to the market. The end result is growing inequality, and the inadequate provision of public services and supports has its inevitable reflection in the social determinants of health.

Income inequality in Canada has increased markedly since 1980. Based on an index of inequality (the Gini coefficient), Canada is currently ranked twentieth of thirty-four OECD nations and twenty-first in terms of the proportion of citizens living in poverty, 11.8 percent.[12] The reduction in inequality from the distributional effects of the tax and benefits systems — which redistribute some income to lower-income people in Canada — fell well behind such efforts in most other OECD nations.[13]

Moreover, among OECD nations, Canada has one of the highest poverty rates for families with children. Indeed, Canada is one of the few nations in which child poverty rates were higher than overall poverty rates over the past two decades. Canada fares even worse in terms of the percentage of workers considered to be low-paid (defined as earning less than two-thirds of the median wage). Canada ranks twentieth of twenty-two nations, with a rate of 22 percent. Compare this standing with Belgium, with 6 percent, and Denmark, with 7.8 percent of employees identified as low-paid.[14]

IMPROVING INCOME DISTRIBUTION

Income and its distribution are strongly shaped by public policy. Governments pass laws and regulations that determine levels not only of minimum wages and employment benefits but also, for those unable to work, unemployment benefits and social assistance rates. Governments also influence income and its distribution by making it easier or more difficult to form unions. Countries that have a greater proportion of their workforce belonging to unions have less income inequality and poverty.[15] Governments also influence income and its distribution through the tax system. More progressive tax systems distribute income and wealth more equitably, which reduces income insecurity and poverty.

Unionized workers have more health and other benefits that provide security

	Medical plan	Dental plan	Life/disability insurance	Pension plan
All employees	57.4%	53.1%	52.5%	43.3%
Unionized	83.7%	76.3%	78.2%	79.9%
Non-unionized	45.4%	42.6%	40.8%	26.6%

Source: A. Jackson, 2010, "The Impact of Unions," in Work and Labour in Canada: Critical Issues, second edition, Canadian Scholars' Press.

The labour movement has an impact on income and income distribution in numerous ways. Unionized workers earn higher wages and have more benefits than do non-unionized workers. The corporate and business community directly influences income distribution through the wages and benefits that it provides employees. It also shapes income and income distribution through its influence on government policy-making with respect to the tax system, labour regulations and general social policy in a whole range of income-related issues. In Canada, business community recommendations concerning these issues lead to greater income and wealth inequalities and increased citizen insecurity.

Anti-poverty groups such as Campaign 2000, Make Poverty History and the Canadian Association of Food Banks have all put forth recommendations for making the distribution of income more equitable. These organizations urge an increase in the minimum wage and a boost in assistance levels for those unable to work, measures that would provide immediate benefits for people who are at the bottom of the income distribution ladder. They also call for increased child benefits similar to levels provided in other nations. Another way of reducing income and wealth inequalities is to make it easier for workplaces to unionize.

Decent social assistance levels decrease income inequality

Bolsa Familia (Family Grant), a Brazilian social program started in 2003, hands out cash to poor families, very poor families by Canadian standards. The program cost about $11.5 billion in 2013, 0.46% of GDP.

Bolsa Familia grants have two strings tied to them: (1) children in recipient families have to go to public health centres for regular checkups and children have to be in school until they finish high school; (2) the grant goes into a bank account of the designated woman of the family who is given a debit card to use the money. It is guaranteed to the families — gives them certainty, the ability to plan their finances (a regular income to budget with). 75% of adult recipients work, 50% of total recipients do not because they are under 14 years old.

Between 2003, when it started, and 2009, incomes of the poorest grew at seven times the rate of incomes of the richest Brazilians. Infant mortality decreased by 40%, school enrolment for the poor sits at 100% — children in Bolsa families graduate at twice the rate of non-Bolsa families.

Source: Stephanie Nolan, 2013, "What Would Robin Hood Do?" Globe and Mail, December 2.

Creating a fairer tax system would help halt the growth of income inequality in Canada. Tax policy over the past two decades has increased the tax burden of lower- and middle-class Canadians, while reducing the taxes for the most well-off. In 1990 the total tax burden of the bottom 10 percent of income earners was 25.5 percent of broad income, including market investments and benefits; that figure increased to 30.7 percent in 2005. In contrast, the top 1 percent of earners saw their total taxes reduced from 34.2 percent to 30.5 percent over the same period; the next highest 4 percent saw a reduction from 36.5 percent to 33.8 percent.[16]

UNEMPLOYMENT AND EMPLOYMENT SECURITY

Canada's unemployment rate of 7.0 percent in 2014 was slightly below the OECD average, giving it a rank of eighteenth of thirty-four OECD nations. More importantly, on the OECD measurement of employment protection regulations for both regular and temporary employment, Canada placed thirty-third out of thirty-four nations. In terms of protection for workers on temporary contracts, Canada tied with the U.S.[17]

This abysmal picture of employment protection compares with Canada's meagre allocations for "active labour policy" — which is public policy that strives to reduce unemployment through employment training and upgrading. Active labour policy is especially important in times of changing employment patterns as a result of increasing economic globalization. On its active labour policy Canada is ranked twentieth among OECD nations.[18]

IMPROVING EMPLOYMENT SECURITY

Job security can be improved in a number of ways, including through research and education, cultural and organizational change, policy and legislation, and reducing inequalities in influence and power. In the realm of research and education, information should be generated and disseminated that will help to develop new ways of thinking about the health and productivity effects of various management strategies. Strategies that create insecure work may appear to promote competitiveness in the short term, but they can have harmful effects on workers' health and a negative impact on productivity in the longer term. According to researchers Tompa, Polanyi and Foley, "There is a particular need to dispel the assumption that cost-cutting and flexible staffing necessarily lead to economic competitiveness."

In the area of cultural change, both the people within organizations and those outside them have to think differently about work and its effects on health. To develop a new way of thinking about health, "workers, employers, government officials, researchers, and others need to come together to develop a shared vision of healthy and productive work."[19]

In terms of institutional change, national governments should work to encourage economic pressures that will facilitate the development of "high-road" instead of "low-road" innovation. In this regard, a long-discussed proposal has been the enactment of international agreements that would provide basic standards of employment and work. Rather than a focus on "free trade," the focus should be on "fair trade."

Governments and companies can work together to develop policy to spread risk and insecurity among governments, employers and employees to reduce the health effects of these changes while at the same time enhancing competitiveness: "This can be achieved through a mix of levers such as macroeconomic policy, education and training policy, regulation of workplace practices and benefits, and policies supportive of various forms of worker empowerment through organization and representation."

In the European Union (E.U.), much more effort is being made to reduce insecurity among workers. In the E.U., job-security laws limit employers' power to lay-off long-tenure workers and also limit renewals of temporary contracts. Higher minimum-pay levels are mandated, and more widespread collective bargaining leads to higher wages and benefits. In Canada, the lack of legislation on these issues means there are far larger pay gaps between precarious and core workers than in most E.U. countries.[20]

Finally, there is power imbalance between employees and employers, although that imbalance varies across occupational and social groups. Employment equity, for example, is still not the standard in Canada: women, Indigenous people and people of colour do not have equal opportunities in hiring, pay, training and advancement. "Consistent with the notion of reducing inequalities, the requirement of certain accommodations for health conditions would allow freer labour-force participation for older individuals and individuals with functional deficits."[21]

EMPLOYMENT AND WORKING CONDITIONS

Working conditions, benefits and opportunities for advancement are strongly related to whether workers are covered by collective agreements and employed in unionized workplaces. Compared to workers in other wealthy countries, Canadian workers are less likely to have their wages and working conditions set by collective agreements. Canada's collective agreement rate is 31.6 percent, giving it a rank of twenty-sixth out of thirty-four OECD nations.[22]

Collective agreements are not only commonplace among the Nordic nations, where union membership is very high, but also among continental European nations. This is because the business sector in the E.U. recognizes the need to work with governments and labour to ensure that workers are able to experience a decent quality of life. Although union membership is lower than in the Nordic nations, the unions in other European countries tend to be very militant. Such co-operation among business, labour and governments is less likely in nations identified as liberal political economies, such as the United Kingdom, United States, Canada and New Zealand.

IMPROVING WORKING CONDITIONS

There are two key actions necessary to improve working conditions in Canada. The first is making more information available: Statistics Canada needs to carry out ongoing surveys about working conditions and practices. Without this kind of information, it is difficult to formulate appropriate responses.

Second, governments must intervene to improve workplace conditions. To this end, numerous official bodies have made recommendations over the years. The Donner Task Force (*Report of the Advisory Group on Working Time and Redistribution of Work*) and the *Report of the Collective Reflection on the Changing Workplace*, for example, called for action not only to "regulate working time by limiting long hours and by making precarious work more secure" but also to implement changes to employment standards and to enhance collective representation of workers. The report of a federal task force on employment standards, *Fairness at Work: Federal Labour Standards for the 21st Century*, called for "limits on long working-time and arbitrary work schedules, more paid time off the job, and measures to secure respect for human rights in the workplace."[23]

Union workers enjoy many advantages

Union	Non-union
You have a legally binding contract that guarantees your rights, working conditions, job security, paid holidays, wages and benefits.	The employer can make promises but is under no obligation to fulfill them. It is difficult to enforce employment standards.
You cannot be fired without just cause and your union will fight to enforce this right.	The employer can fire you at any time with no reason even if you do good work. If you fight for what you deserve you can lose your job.
With each round of negotiations, your union achieves higher wages and better working conditions for you.	Raises and promotions are few and far between and completely up to the discretion of management where favouritism can play a major role.
You have the grievance procedure to fight against unfair treatment, poor working conditions or anything else that violates your collective agreement or the provincial Human Rights Code.	The employer can force you to work in unsafe conditions and change the pace or requirements of your job with no warning and no consequence. Harassment and discrimination rarely get challenged.
Your contract provides excellent benefits, including life insurance, hospital care, vision and dental care, disability benefits and pension plans — all without additional costs to you.	The employer decides on benefits and often they cost you extra money. In addition, these benefits can be changed or taken away with no notice.

Source: United Food and Commercial Workers Union, 2016, Benefits of Union Membership *<http://tinyurl.com/hmmj9az>*

Making it easier for workers to organize is essential because "it is unlikely that there will be significant positive changes in the workplace if everything is left to employers, and if governments do not help equalize bargaining power between workers and employers."[24] About 30 percent of Canadian workers are members of unions, and the magnitude of differences between unionized and non-unionized workplaces is striking. Employees who work under collective agreements negotiated by unions receive numerous benefits and have a greater ability to influence working conditions. Unionized workers covered under collective agreements enjoy higher wages. While benefits are seen across all occupations, the union advantage is especially great for blue-collar and mainly low-wage private services.[25]

Unionized workplaces lead to increased power for employees in relation to the employer, greater opportunities for training and advancement, and greater productivity. Internationally, countries with a higher incidence of unionized workplaces also show less income inequality, lower poverty rates and fewer incidences of lower-paying jobs. Canada has one of the highest rates of low-paid workers (22 percent) — defined as earning less than two-thirds of the median national full-time wage — among a number of wealthy developed nations.[26]

EDUCATION

In 2012, Canada spent 5 percent of GDP on education overall, which placed it eleventh among thirty-three OECD nations. Taking just primary and secondary education into account, Canada did less well, spending 3.2 percent of its GDP, giving it a rank of twentieth, and post-secondary spending, at 1.7 percent, placed Canada at fourth among twenty-eight OECD nations.[27] Where people have good jobs and decent incomes, their children's educational outcomes improve. This is a well-known dynamic, but higher levels of education are also necessary for access to good jobs and decent incomes. We do know how to improve education outcomes.

IMPROVING EDUCATION

Expanding educational opportunities generally is the most effective way to improve access to education. We need to see this as a public, not an individual and private, concern (if for no other reason than the returns on education spending are clear in the savings on health and other social costs of poor education), and education must be a lifelong enterprise.

Barbara Ronson McNichol and Irving Rootman propose that governments improve the education system for young people and develop an effective adult education and training system. Much of this would involve intersectionality, meaning that different sectors work together to support Canadians in their education across the lifecourse.

> For example, many schools are empty after school and on weekends while children and youth in the neighbourhood have no safe places to play and no constructive activities to do. Many recreation centres now charge user fees, which discourage participation of at-risk children and youth who are most in need of constructive outlets.[28]

Urban Circle Training Centre, in Winnipeg's inner city, illustrates the success of such programs. It has about 150 students at any given time, and its success rate — students graduating and finding a job or going on to further education — is 85–90 percent. This program's success at moving young adults from social assistance (and worse) to jobs saved governments an estimated $53.5 million between 1990 and 2010.[29] Governments should also commit to policy and funding to ensure that adults have access to a variety of literacy and learning opportunities in their home communities. Governments also need to fund projects aimed at increasing the accessibility of information.

EARLY CHILD DEVELOPMENT

Along with Canada's child poverty rate, which is amongst the highest of OECD nations, the country is also among the worst in meeting early child education and care benchmarks. Canadian families do not have access to regulated child-care spaces, which is not surprising given that Canada spends the lowest proportion of national resources on early child education and care among wealthy developed nations. Canada's spending exceeds only that of Greece.[30]

Early child development is influenced by government support of families, the strength of the labour movement and access to a living wage. But Canada is increasingly being recognized as a child-unfriendly nation. That the country has one of the highest proportions of children living in poverty is largely due to the high proportion of low-paid workers: Canada's minimum wages, replacement benefits during unemployment and social assistance benefits are amongst the lowest of the wealthy nations.[31]

IMPROVING EARLY CHILD DEVELOPMENT

People whose workplaces are covered by union-negotiated collective agreements fare somewhat better than non-union members in terms of their income situation. In nations with strong union memberships, child poverty rates are much lower.[32] And, not surprisingly, infant mortality and low birth-weight rates – important indicators of health – are much better.

Important segments of the corporate and business community, in the form of some of its largest and most influential organizations, have strongly opposed increasing the wages and benefits available to families with children. To give just one example, in a brief presented to the Newfoundland and Labrador 2008 Minimum Wage Review, the Newfoundland and Labrador Business Coalition, made up of members of a variety of business sectors, opposed the provincial government's proposal to raise the minimum wage to $10 an hour.[33]

Similarly, through their strong — and mostly successful — efforts to reduce the extent of government tax revenues, business organizations — together with conservative organizations such as the Canadian Taxpayers Federation and the Fraser and C.D. Howe institutes — have made it difficult for governments to support families with children through the provision of family-related benefits and early child education and care programs. An improvement in the quality of early child development would have health repercussions for Canadians across the socio-economic spectrum, from the most vulnerable members of society to well-off Canadians.

In addition to providing a universal and affordable child-care system,

A $7 revolution

In Quebec, all parents pay the same child-care rate of $7 per child per day. In other provinces child-care can be as much as $2000 per month ($100 per day). The Quebec government spends $2.2 billion per year on this program (nearly two-thirds of the $3.6 billion spent by all provinces and territories combined), about 0.7% of GDP. The OECD recommends 1% as the minimum for a good quality child-care system. Begun in fall of 1997, the program also includes expanded childbirth leave, including five weeks exclusively for fathers, full-day kindergarten and after-school care. The labour-force participation rate of women aged 25-44 years went from nearly the lowest in Canada (after for Atlantic provinces) to the highest in the country. The number of single parents on welfare was cut in half, and after-tax income rose by 81%. Over a sixteen-year period the rate of child poverty was reduced by half.

Source: Erin Anderssen and Kim Mackrael, 2013, "A $7 Revolution," Globe and Mail, October 19.

proposals for improving early child development are virtually the same as those for reducing poverty in general and child poverty in particular. These include making it easier to unionize workplaces, raising minimize wages and developing a national housing and food security program. Not only are the recommendations similar to those of many Canadian policy organizations concerned with these issues, they are also similar to the policy directions that have been effective in bettering early child development in other wealthy industrial nations.[34]

FOOD SECURITY

The percentage of Canadians experiencing food insecurity is just over 11 percent. In Australia and the United Kingdom, food insecurity (called food poverty in the U.K.) is estimated at 5 percent. Not surprisingly, the figure for the United States is 12.6 percent. In New Zealand it is a striking 20 percent.[35]

IMPROVING FOOD SECURITY

If public policy is to fully address food insecurity, the first item on the agenda must be to ensure an increase in the incomes of those experiencing food insecurity, which means, as a start, increasing minimum wages and social assistance rates. Governments must also make sure that healthy foods, especially staples such as milk, are affordable. Lynn McIntyre and Laura Anderson assert:

> Currently, there is little action being taken in the Canadian policy arena to address household food insecurity. Food-based responses such as food banks and community kitchens are unable to address the real problem of household food insecurity: that households cannot afford to buy their own food.[36]

In relation to food security, the availability of affordable housing has to be a key governmental priority. Too often families are forced to decide between paying the rent or feeding the kids. A lack of affordable child-care is another barrier that often keeps mothers out of the workforce: a universal, publicly funded (which means affordable) child-care system must be set in place. Governments should also expand programs that have been shown to reduce poverty and food insecurity, providing an integrated slate of work-related supports, health and recreation provision, and other transition assistance.

Some efforts to address food insecurity as a cause of poor health have had some success. In Toronto, healthy family teams that include doctors are "prescribing income" by helping poor patients navigate government social service bureaucracies. In the United States, the Fruit and Vegetable Prescription Program promotes partnerships between heath care and local food providers to find solutions to diet-related illnesses, and the United Nations recommends taxing and regulating unhealthy foods. At the community level, retail co-ops can reduce food prices, particularly for remote communities but also through the co-op model of users as owners. Profits stay in communities, rather than go to distant corporations, which helps communities to improve local well-being. Finally, calls for a national food strategy based on food sovereignty is an attempt to integrate agriculture with food security. Groups like the People's Food Project, Food Secure Canada and the National Farmer's Union have campaigns that include a call to entrench the right to healthy food into the Canadian constitution. Loosening agriculture from an industrial and corporate model are key elements of providing food security.[37]

HOUSING

Canada is the only developed nation that does not have a national housing policy. Prior to 1993, through the Central Mortgage and Housing Corporation, Canada supported low-cost housing by, in part, funding non-profit and cooperative housing. By 1993, there were over 650,000 units of social housing in Canada, in about 6 percent of the occupied dwellings. Since then the national stock of social housing has dwindled to under 500,000 units, even though the total number of units needed is growing. Canada now spends 0.3 percent of its GDP on housing, which gives it a rank of eleventh out of thirty-four OECD nations. The country faces a severe crisis of housing affordability.[38]

IMPROVING HOUSING SECURITY AND REDUCING HOMELESSNESS

A 2015 report by the Federation of Canadian Municipalities (FCM), *Built to Last: Strengthening the Foundations of Housing in Canada,* outlines the following recommendations to address the housing crisis in Canada.[39]

Stimulate market and affordable rental construction
The FCM is calling for federal tax incentives aimed at removing barriers to new affordable and market-rental housing, including a rental incentive tax credit. To stop the serious erosion — through demolition and conversion to condominiums — of existing lower-rent properties, this incentive would credit property owners for selling affordable assets to eligible non-profit providers (including a municipality), thereby preserving assets and promoting long-term affordability. The credit would target small investors that face large tax liabilities when they sell properties.

Preserve and renew federal investments in social housing
to rebalance the fiscal burden between the federal
government and provincial/territorial governments

The FCM is calling for the federal government to recommit to its current level of investment as a fixed contribution to the F/P/T partnership, to sustain and preserve Canada's existing social housing stock of 600,000 lower-rent homes reserved for households in need.

Develop a supporting framework for strategies to fight homelessness

The FCM is calling for current allotments of $253 million annually to the federal investment in the Affordable Housing program and the $119 million annually for the Homelessness Partnering Strategy to be renewed and made permanent when they expire in 2019. The FCM is also calling for further collaborations across governments for appropriate funding to ensure that rental subsidies are made available, to ensure that persons and families exiting from homelessness can be affordably stabilized in permanent housing.

The Liberal government elected in 2015 is promising action on providing affordable housing for Canadians. This could be done by reconstituting the role of the Canada Mortgage and Housing Corporation (CMHC) in planning, funding and monitoring a social housing policy. The CMHC should facilitate knowledge-sharing between all levels of government, leading to concrete local plans that promote a diversity of ownership/tenure models (individual owner, private renting, non-profit and co-op housing) and resume its former role of funding social housing.[40] The questions are will the federal government meet these commitments and will these commitments be enough to address the housing crisis in Canada.

SOCIAL EXCLUSION

As we've seen, when it comes to their employment situations and wages, Indigenous and other racialized groups, women and people with disabilities fare poorly as compared to the rest of Canadians.

Martin Cooke and his colleagues calculated Human Development Index (HDI) scores for Indigenous peoples in Australia, Canada, New Zealand and the United States and compared these to non-Indigenous peoples in these nations and to other nations' overall scores. HDI scores consist of an equal weighting of life expectancy, educational participation and adult literacy rates, with GDP per capita in constant dollars. While Canada ranked eighth overall in HDI scores, the index score for Indigenous peoples ranked Canada at thirty-third.[41]

The 2007 United Nations Declaration on the Rights of Indigenous Peoples identifies numerous areas in which national governments could work to better the situation of Indigenous peoples. The Declaration includes articles concerned with improving economic and social conditions, the right to attain the highest levels of health and the right to protect and conserve their environments. Sadly, Canada was one of the few nations to initially vote against its adoption, but Canada eventually ratified the Declaration in 2012.[42]

The 1996 Royal Commission on Indigenous Peoples (RCAP) included the following policy recommendations:

- legislation, including a new Royal Proclamation stating Canada's commitment to a new relationship and companion legislation setting out a treaty process and recognition of Indigenous nations and governments;
- recognition of an Indigenous order of government, subject to the Charter of Rights and Freedoms, with authority over matters related to the good government and welfare of

United Nations Declaration on the Rights of Indigenous Peoples

Article 1

Indigenous peoples have the right to the full enjoyment, as a collective or as individuals, of all human rights and fundamental freedoms as recognized in the Charter of the United Nations, the Universal Declaration of Human Rights and international human rights law.

Article 2

Indigenous peoples and individuals are free and equal to all other peoples and individuals and have the right to be free from any kind of discrimination, in the exercise of their rights, in particular that based on their indigenous origin or identity.

Article 3

Indigenous peoples have the right to self-determination. By virtue of that right they freely determine their political status and freely pursue their economic, social and cultural development.

Article 4

Indigenous peoples, in exercising their right to self-determination, have the right to autonomy or self-government in matters relating to their internal and local affairs, as well as ways and means for financing their autonomous functions.

Article 5

Indigenous peoples have the right to maintain and strengthen their distinct political, legal, economic, social and cultural institutions, while retaining their right to participate fully, if they so choose, in the political, economic, social and cultural life of the State.

Source: United Nations, 2007 <ohchr.org/english/issues/indigenous/declaration.htm>.

Indigenous peoples and their territories;
- replacement of the federal Department of Indian Affairs with two departments, one to implement the new relationship with Indigenous nations and one to provide services for non-self-governing communities;
- creation of an Indigenous Parliament;
- expansion of the Indigenous land and resource base;
- recognition of Métis self-government, provision of a land base, and recognition of Métis rights to hunt and fish on Crown land;
- initiatives to address social, education, health, and housing needs, including the training of ten thousand health professionals over a ten-year period, the establishment of an Indigenous peoples' university, and recognition of Indigenous nations' authority over child welfare.[43]

Yet, as Smylie and Firestone point out, the current state of inaction on these recommendations is striking. Since the release of the RCAP report, there has been "some slow progress in the area of Indigenous-controlled health services, as well as the identification of Indigenous health human resources." To Canada's great shame, they note:

> However, more generally, the Canadian government's lack of implementation of the RCAP recommendations has been extensively criticized by national and international human rights bodies, including the Canadian Human Rights Commission, the United Nations Human Rights Committee, and the United Nations Committee on Economic, Social, and Cultural Rights.[44]

In the past, immigrants to Canada would gradually reach income and employment levels comparable to the Canadian-born, but this is no longer happening. Statistics Canada has documented differences in income and employment status of recent and earlier immigrants to Canada.[45] In recent years, immigrants in all education and age groups, including the university-educated, increasingly have low-incomes. Given that 75 percent of recent immigrants are members of racialized groups, it appears that racism and discrimination are responsible for these diminishing returns.

The Truth and Reconciliation Commission and Health

In 2015, the Truth and Reconciliation Commission (TRC) released 94 recommendations in its "Call to Action." Seven of these recommendations are specific to health. These recommendations build on those of the RCAP and call for explicit acknowledgement of causal links between current Indigenous health challenges in Canada and federal government policies including residential schools, as well as the recognition and upholding of Indigenous rights to health care.

The TRC also advocates for the co-development with Indigenous peoples of measureable goals setting and progress reporting in order to close health equity gaps; a resolution of jurisdiction disputes through the recognition and address of the distinct health needs of Métis, Inuit and off-reserve peoples; respect for Indigenous healing practices; sustainable funding for new and existing Indigenous healing centres; and increase in Indigenous health professionals and cultural competency training for all health care professionals.

Source. J. Smylie and M. Firestone, 2016, "The Health of Indigenous People," in D. Raphael (ed.), Social Determinants of Health: Canadian Perspectives, third edition, Canadian Scholars' Press.

We need, among other things, opportunities for foreign-trained professionals to practise their professions in Canada. We also need strong enforcement of anti-discrimination laws. Given that people of colour are especially vulnerable to difficult living circumstances, which have an undoubted impact on the social determinants of health, we especially need our governments at all levels to take an active role in addressing these issues.

GENDER

In measurements of women's wages as a percentage of men's, in 2013 Canada ranked twenty-eighth out of thirty-four OECD nations, showing a gender wage gap of 19 percent. On the United Nation's measure of gender inequality index in 2014, Canada ranked twenty-fifth among wealthy developed nations.[46]

Governments, health authorities, non-governmental organizations and advocacy groups have outlined various strategies to address women's health issues. These solutions usually focus on aspects of health care and health outcomes such as reproductive health, screening for various forms of cancer and appropriate prescribing of medications. They tend not to address the social and economic structures that shape women's health:

Action on these more deeply embedded elements of the social structure may require action far beyond the health sector. Moreover, such strategies need to be developed with an awareness of women's lives so that women are truly able to benefit from the initiative. Financial support for caregiving, for example, is currently part of the Employment Insurance scheme in Canada. Unfortunately, access to this program is limited to people who work full-time, and therefore many of the people who need this assistance the most—women—are unable to access the program because they do not qualify.[47]

Many of the recommendations provided in this chapter for the other issues are also pertinent to addressing women's inequality.

Canada's gender wage gap is higher than in many countries

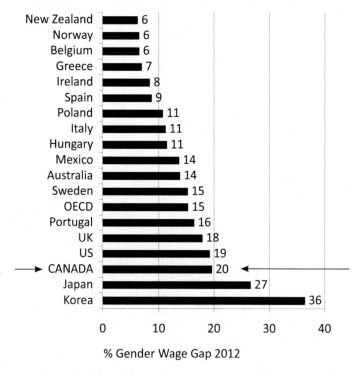

% Gender Wage Gap 2012

Source: Organisation for Economic Cooperation and Development, 2016, Gender Wage Gap *<oecd. org/gender/data/genderwagegap.htm>.*

These suggestions include the provision of living wages and adequate social assistance benefits, affordable housing and child-care, and adjustments to make it easier to qualify for employment insurance. For example, the Manitoba's Women's Health Strategy has identified affordable housing as one way to improve the health of women.[48] Women especially benefit when they are employed in unionized workplaces. Making it easier to organize workplaces would go a long way to improve the situation of women in Canada. On the work front, ensuring pay equity and combating discrimination in the workplace are also important means of overcoming the negative results of the social determinants of health for women.

Connecting all these issues has to be efforts to deal with violence against women. The same dynamic that condones or ignores violence against women prevents them from acquiring living wages, pay equity and so on. So, campaigns that draw attention to the continuing violence are an important step forward. Two examples are the Manitoba Status of Women's partnership with the Winnipeg Blue Bombers on a pubic relations campaign showing the role men can take in preventing violence, and the federal government's inquiry into the hundreds of cases of missing and murdered Indigenous women.

DISABILITY

Disability-related public policy can be divided into policies that improve benefits and policies that improve integration. Benefits-related policy refers to the accessibility and generosity of benefits available to persons with disabilities, and integration-related policy refers to the extent to which persons with disabilities are provided with opportunities to participate in paid employment. Canada ranks amongst the lowest in benefit provision to people with disabilities and is well below the average in integration policy. Moreover, Canada is amongst the lowest spenders in what the OECD calls "incapacity spending," which refers to all the monies made available to provide benefits to persons with disabilities or to assist them in gaining employment.

The Council of Canadians with Disabilities published a framework for a national action plan for improving the lives of people living with disabilities. The plan includes the following areas of action:

New investments in disability related supports
Properly executed new investments can bring change to the lives of people with disabilities. An appropriately targeted investment in disability-related supports would assist Canadians with disabilities to participate in early learning and child-care, become educated and employed, live more independently, and look after their families. ...

New initiatives to alleviate poverty
The poverty of Canadians with disabilities is a national disgrace. Canadians with disabilities and their families are twice as likely to live in poverty as other Canadians and the incidence of poverty among Aboriginal People with disabilities is even higher. Existing systems of income support are failing Canadians with disabilities. The Government of Canada must commit to addressing poverty and reforming Canada's income support programs for Canadians with disabilities. ...

New supports to increase access to labour-force participation
Through Advantage Canada and the recent budget, the Government of Canada committed to increasing access to

training, education, accommodation and labour market attachment for people with disabilities....

New initiatives to promote access, inclusion and full citizenship
To achieve positive outcomes within the building blocks of employment, income and disability supports, investments are also needed in other related and complementary areas.[49]

In relation to the last action area, the Council recommends government committment to addressing the following (among others): transportation; the UN Convention on the Rights of Persons with Disabilities; accessible technology; support disability community knowledge mobilization and knowledge transfer; and re-establish a specific parliamentary committee on the status of Canadians with disabilities.

SOCIAL SAFETY NET

Given all of findings presented in this book, it is not at all surprising that Canada also does very poorly when it comes to our much-vaunted social safety net. Canada performs poorly in terms of the social assistance benefits provided to those who are unable to work. Canada's social assistance for a single person is ranked thirty-seventh of forty-three OECD nations. At a level of 22 percent of the median income, the level of benefits is less than half of the poverty line, which is regarded as 50 percent of median income. For a couple with two children, the level is 35 percent of median income, a full 15 percent below the poverty line. This gives Canada a rank of twenty-third among developed nations.[50]

HEALTH CARE SERVICES

Canada's public spending on health care as a percentage of GDP was 7.2 percent in 2013, for a rank of fourteenth out of thirty-four OECD nations. Since public spending on health care is reflected in public health care coverage, it is not surprising that ten of the thirteen higher-spending nations cover a greater proportion of health care costs than our system does.

In fact, out of the thirty-four OECD nations, twenty-one countries cover a greater proportion of total health care costs than does Canada. The percentage of health care costs covered by Canada's medicare system is only 71 percent. The health care systems of the Netherlands, the U.K., Norway, Denmark, Czech Republic, Sweden, Japan, Luxembourg and Iceland cover more than 80 percent of health care costs, and the Czech Republic, Luxembourg and Iceland do so at less cost than Canada.[51]

GOVERNMENTS, MARKETS AND HEALTH

For many Canadians the social determinants of health have an adverse impact because of how the economic system acts to distribute resources so unequally. In addition, governments make matters worse by leaving what should be public policy — distribution of income and wealth and the provision of benefits, supports and services — to the market to determine. Compared to other wealthy developed nations, Canada falls far behind in managing its economic system in a way that provides citizens with a higher and more equitable quality of life, health and well-being.

Short of a radical restructuring of our market-dominated socio-economic system, governments can do many things to deal with these deficiencies. The actions that would strengthen the social determinants of health fall into three main areas: policies to reduce the incidence of lower-income, policies to reduce social exclusion and policies to strengthen Canada's social infrastructure.

Policies to reduce the incidence of low income
- raise the minimum wage to a living wage,
- improve pay equity,
- restore and improve income supports for those unable to gain employment,
- provide a guaranteed minimum income.

Policies to reduce social exclusion
- enforce legislation that protects the rights of minority groups, particularly concerning employment rights and anti-discrimination,
- ensure that families have sufficient income to provide their children with the means of attaining healthy development,
- reduce inequalities in income and wealth within the population through progressive taxation of income and inherited wealth,
- assure access to education, training and employment opportunities, especially for the long-term unemployed,
- remove barriers to health and social services, which involves understanding where and why such barriers exist,
- provide adequate follow-up support for those leaving institutional care,
- create housing policies that provide enough affordable housing of reasonable standard,
- institute employment policies that preserve and create jobs,
- direct attention to the health needs of immigrants and to the unfavourable socio-economic position of many groups,

including the particular difficulties that many new Canadians face in accessing health and other care services.

Policies to strengthen Canada's social infrastructure
- restore health and service program spending to the average level of OECD nations,
- develop a national housing strategy and allocate an additional 1 percent of federal spending for affordable housing,
- provide a national daycare program,
- provide a national pharmacare program,
- restore eligibility for and the level of employment benefits to previous levels,
- require that provincial social assistance programs be accessible and funded at levels to ensure health,
- ensure that supports are available to support Canadians through critical life transitions.[52]

These are all public policy goals that can be achieved. All we need is the political will to carry them out. This project will only come about if the public mobilizes in support of these efforts.

WHAT NEEDS TO BE DONE?

We need to reclaim equality as a positive social value — it
has gone out of fashion in recent decades, having been
squelched in the pursuit of free enterprise. The values of
the marketplace — individual greed, fear, insecurity — tri-
umphed, and our rich legacy of social values — compassion,
caring, sharing — were demeaned. The pertinent question
is: What values shall govern Canada? —David Langille,
political economist[1]

Public policies that would more equitably distribute economic
and social resources in Canada will strengthen the social
determinants of health. Such public policies are not pipe
dreams: they have been implemented to good effect in many wealthy
developed nations, most of which are not as wealthy as Canada.

It is commonly argued that these nations accomplish public
policies that promote the SDoH at the expense of economic performance. In fact, the opposite is true. The Conference Board of Canada
analyzed the performance of several wealthy industrialized nations
based on indicators of health (e.g., life expectancy, infant mortality),

education (e.g., high school and education completion, achieve-ment scores), environment (e.g., emissions, water quality), society (e.g., disabled income, elderly and child poverty, income inequality, gender income gap and voter turnout), economy (e.g., income per capita, GDP growth) and knowledge innovation (e.g., patents). The Board found that social-democratic nations (for example, Denmark, Finland, Norway and Sweden) — the ones whose public policies pay the greatest attention to the SDoH — not only outperform Canada on most health and society indicators, but also out-perform Canada on knowledge innovation indicators and do as well or better on many economic indicators.[2]

We can learn from these nations with a public policy approach to improving the social determinant of health. There are also lessons from our own past. The twenty-five years of Canada's history after World War II saw the implementation of medicare, public pensions, unemployment insurance and federal and provincial programs that delivered affordable housing to Canadians. These public policies promoted health and prevented illness.

Since the 1980s Canada has moved away from providing citizens with these means of maintaining their health. Politicians and policy-makers are well aware of this trend and the possibilities for a different approach. Canadian government documents and reports have been putting forth social determinants of health ideas since the mid-1970s, yet Canada is now a laggard on the SDoH front. Much of this has to do with Canadian governments heartily taking to the ideology of neoliberalism. As a consequence, they have been giving in to the demands of the corporate and business community to reduce the role of government in managing the economy and providing Canadians with economic and social security.

If Canada is to return to a public policy pathway that provides high quality and equitably distributed SDoH, we have to build strong social and political movements that literally *force* governments and policy-makers to enact health-supporting measures. Governments must come to understand that they are out of step with the needs and desires of the citizens of Canada. A SDoH approach — which is about egalitarianism and collective responsibility to one another — will create the kind of society most Canadians want to live in. If governments fail to take this approach, we can remove them from office through the electoral process and replace them with governments that will.

MOVING FORWARD

Our governments will pay more attention to developing public policies that recognize the importance of the SDoH if they believe public opinion is in favour of such action. It may be that Canadians actually understand the connections as they live them, but other public voices proclaiming non-SDoH approaches are louder and get more air time. The lack of public voice to these issues is due to governments, public health agencies, the media and disease associations proclaiming messages that reflect their preoccupation with medical and individual lifestyle approaches to health and illness.

Even so, there is an impressive number of university-based researchers, research institutes and local public health units across Canada looking at health issues from a SDoH perspective.[3] Yet their voices are not being heard by the public. It also seems there is a conspiracy to keep this information under wraps. Perhaps powerful economic and political interests that benefit from neglecting the SDoH are able to shape how we as a society conceive of health and the means of promoting it. This leads to the question of who is benefiting from growing inequalities in income and wealth at the expense of the SDoH. David Langille suggests:

The erosion of Canada's social and economic well-being over the last four decades was the deliberate outcome of strategies designed to roll back the welfare state and restore corporate profits. Increasingly, Canadian public policy has been moulded to the needs of the transnational corporations. Regulations were reduced and trade barriers removed, forcing firms and individuals to become more "competitive" in order to survive in the global market economy. That explains the deterioration of our quality of life and quality of jobs, the erosion of our health care and education systems amidst increasing insecurity, inequality, militarism, and state surveillance.[4]

Despite this lack of attention in the public sphere, increasing numbers of community-oriented organizations and agencies in Canada are adopting a SDoH perspective. These include the Canadian Medical Association, Canadian Nurses Association, Canadian Association of Social Workers, Canadian Mental Health Association, Canadian

Cultural hegemony and the neglect of the SDoH
Cultural hegemony, a concept developed by Italian scholar and activist Antonio Gramsci, refers to domination, or rule, achieved through ideas and the culture of a society. In other words, particular groups of people who have power within social institutions are able to strongly influence the everyday thoughts, expectations and behaviour of others by directing the ideas, values and beliefs that become the dominant worldview of a society.

Source: About Education, 2015, Cultural Hegemony <sociology.about.com/od/C_Index/fl/Cultural-Hegemony.htm>.

Psychological Association, Canadian Public Health Association, YWCA, YMCA, and many, many more. They do so because the evidence of the importance of the social determinants of health to their clients is so compelling it cannot be ignored. These organizations and agencies must be encouraged to not only continue their efforts, but to kick up their efforts to embrace advocacy and to directly question current public policy.

An agenda that promotes improved SDoH will be translated into health-supporting public policies through two main and interacting avenues: education and mobilization. Canadians need to pressure governments and policy-makers to refocus their efforts in a different direction — towards strengthening the quality of the SDoH and making their distribution more equitable. Part of that mobilization is supporting political candidates who are receptive to the SDoH approach. These candidates can likely be found in every political party, but are more likely to be found and influenced in some political parties than others. Those genuinely interested in these ideas should be supported, and those who are not must be educated and pressured to adopt this focus.

Canadians can act to implement a SDoH agenda as individuals or through support of and/or membership in advocacy groups. As individuals or members of advocacy groups, people can influence governments and policy-makers directly through lobbying activities or indirectly through ongoing public education on the importance of the SDoH.

We must also pressure the specific institutions with influence on governments and policy-makers. These institutions include local and provincial public health units, disease associations and their affiliates, and the media. Given their mandates of promoting the public's health, preventing disease and informing their readership, there is every good reason that these institutions should be part of a SDoH movement.

EDUCATING ABOUT SDOH

Canadians are generally uninformed about the SDoH. When asked in surveys to describe the pathways to good health, Canadians overwhelmingly repeat the healthy-living mantra of nutritious diets, physical activity, rest and avoiding tobacco. In no survey has a majority of Canadians reported *any* social determinant of health as a significant influence upon health. This should not be surprising considering the ongoing barrage of health-lifestyle messages. The media's profound neglect of the SDoH contributes to this lack of knowledge.[5]

How can Canadians be educated about the SDoH? The first step is

Upstream: A national movement to address the SDoH

Upstream is a movement to create a healthy society through evidence-based, people-centred ideas. Upstream seeks to reframe public discourse around addressing the SDoH in order to build a healthier society.

- Upstream works with the growing body of evidence on the SDoH and uses that knowledge to guide recommendations for change.
- By sharing stories through a variety of media, Upstream seeks to creatively engage citizens, sparking within them a personal stake in the SDoH and a demand for upstream alternatives to the status quo.
- Upstream uses this evidence and storytelling to foster a vibrant network of organizations and individuals who share this vision.

By demonstrating that a better way is possible, we can help create the conditions for wiser decisions and a healthier Canada.

Source: Upstream, 2016, A Healthier Society Begins with You *<thinkupstream.net/>.*

In a survey, Canadians were asked to identify the three most important factors that contribute to good health.

Proper Rest
13%

Not Smoking
12%

Diet/Nutrition
82%

Physical Activity
70%

When provided with a list, Canadians were asked to identify social determinants as having a strong or very strong impact on health.

Unemployment
49%

Income Level
33%

Education Level
33%

Childhood Experiences
44%

Quality of Housing
34%

Source: Canadian Population Health Initiative, Select Highlights on Public Views of the Determinants of Health, *CPHI 2004.*

simply to pass the word: we can all tell friends, relatives, neighbours and colleagues. Two messages are central:

1. The primary determinants of health are not the medical treatments we can access or the healthy lifestyle choices we make, but rather the living and working conditions under which we live.
2. These living and working conditions are largely shaped by public policy decisions made by our governments.

A public primer on the SDoH entitled *Social Determinants of Health: The Canadian Facts* is a free online resource that communicates these messages. It has been downloaded over 350,000 times since April 2010, with 85 percent of these downloads made by Canadians. It is being widely used in college and university courses across a range of disciplines.[6]

Alongside word-of-mouth, we should insist that established communication systems that convey "healthy lifestyle" messages shift their messages to the SDoH. Public health units, disease associations and government ministries of health expend tens of millions of dollars annually on such systems. For example, *The 2010 Report on the Integrated Pan-Canadian Healthy Living Strategy* provides a sense of the enormous amount of resources expended in "healthy living" activities in Canada.[7] Instead of providing the worn-out threats to health of tobacco use, unhealthy diets and lack of physical activity, they must be pressured to draw attention to unhealthy and insecure living conditions, unhealthy workplaces and deprived childhoods.

Shifting health messages to a SDoH perspective

The traditional ten tips for better health:

1. Don't smoke. If you can, stop. If you can't, cut down.
2. Follow a balanced diet with plenty of fruit and vegetables.
3. Keep physically active.
4. Manage stress by, for example, talking things through and making time to relax.
5. If you drink alcohol, do so in moderation.
6. Cover up in the sun, and protect children from sunburn.
7. Practise safer sex.
8. Take up cancer-screening opportunities.
9. Be safe on the roads: follow the Highway Code.
10. Learn the First Aid ABCs: airways, breathing, circulation.

The SDoH ten tips for better health:

1. Don't be poor. If you can, stop. If you can't, try not to be poor for long.
2. Don't have poor parents.
3. Be able to own a car.
4. Don't work in a stressful, low-paid manual job.
5. Don't live in damp, low-quality housing.
6. Be able to afford to go on a foreign holiday and sunbathe.
7. Practise not losing your job and don't become unemployed.
8. Take up all benefits you are entitled to, if you are unemployed, retired, sick or disabled.
9. Don't live next to a busy major road or near a polluting factory.
10. Learn how to fill in the complex housing benefit/asylum application forms before you become homeless and destitute.

Source: L. Donaldson, "Ten Tips for Better Health," and D. Gordon, 2009, "An Alternative Ten Tips for Better Health," reprinted in D. Raphael (ed.), Social Determinants of Health. Canadian Perspectives, second edition, Canadian Scholars' Press.

PUBLIC HEALTH UNITS

Public health units — until recently — have been reluctant to communicate information about the SDoH to Canadians. But this may be changing as local public health units across Canada begin to engage in public education about the SDoH. On its own, the Sudbury and District Public Health Unit in Ontario created a video animation *Let's Start a Conversation about Health and Not Talk about Health Care at All,* which does a remarkable job of explaining the SDoH. It has now been adapted for use by no less than twenty other public health units

Let's start a conversation about health and not talk about health care at all

"Health equity means that all people can reach their full health potential and should not be disadvantaged from attaining it because of their race, ethnicity, religion, gender, age, social class, socioeconomic status or other socially determined circumstance." (National Collaborating Centre for Determinants of Health, 2013)

Differences in health that exist between groups of people that are systematic, socially produced and unfair or unjust are defined as **health inequities**.

For example, the rate of obesity in Sudbury's most disadvantaged areas is twice as high than in Sudbury's most advantaged areas. This is a health inequity. No one in our community needs to be at risk of poor health solely due to the social and economic environments they live in.

To learn more about health equity and what impacts our health, watch [our] short video: *Let's Start a Conversation about Health and Not Talk about Health Care at All.*

Source: Sudbury Health District, 2015, "About Health Equity" <sdhu.com/health-topics-programs/ health-equity/health-equity>.

in Ontario (out of the total of thirty-six) and many others across Canada and even in the U.S. and Australia.[8]

Inquire into whether your local public health unit is carrying out messages that promote a SDoH approach. If they are, contact them and thank them for doing so. If they are not, inquire why they are not. If health unit staff are not aware of these concepts, direct them to the available resources. If they are aware of these concepts but have failed to act upon them, direct their attention to public health units applying these concepts in public health practice and demand similar efforts.

DISEASE ASSOCIATIONS

If we just followed the advice of the major disease associations, such as the Heart and Stroke Foundation, Canadian Diabetes Association and Canadian Cancer Society, we would have no sense that economic and social conditions play any role in the incidence of these major diseases. In addition, Canadians are assured by these associations — despite tons of contrary research evidence — that heart disease and stroke, adult-onset diabetes, respiratory disease and many cancers can be averted through the adoption of "healthy lifestyle choices." Even more importantly, Canadians are told that the solutions to these problems will come from medical and behavioural research rather than public policies that improve the quality of the SDoH and make their distribution more equitable.

These disease associations ignore the direct health effects of the SDoH and they also ignore whether "healthy lifestyle choices" are even possible for those most vulnerable to these diseases. Perhaps even more telling is the lack of consistent research evidence that these "healthy lifestyle choices" are reliable predictors of the onset of the chronic diseases, about which Canadians are understandably confused. For example, not eating fruits and vegetables is

Major disease associations that do not use a SDoH approach

Alzheimer Society Canada
Amyotrophic Lateral Sclerosis Society of Canada
Arthritis Society*
Brain Injury Association of Canada*
Canadian Breast Cancer Foundation
Canadian Cancer Society*
Canadian Cystic Fibrosis Foundation
Canadian Diabetes Association*
Canadian Foundation for AIDS Research*
Canadian Hospice Palliative Care Association
Canadian Liver Foundation*
Canadian Lung Association*
Canadian Mental Health Association*
Canadian Orthopaedic Foundation
Crohn's and Colitis Foundation of Canada
Easter Seals Canada
Foundation Fighting Blindness–Canada
Heart and Stroke Foundation of Canada*
Huntington Society of Canada
Kidney Cancer Canada
Lupus Canada*
Kidney Foundation of Canada*
Mood Disorders Society of Canada*
Muscular Dystrophy Canada
Multiple Sclerosis Society of Canada
Osteoporosis Canada*
Ovarian Cancer Canada
Parkinson Society Canada
SMARTRISK*
Spina Bifida and Hydrocephalus Association of Canada

Note: (* illness strongly associated with SDoH).

sometimes found to be related to cardiovascular disease but not cancer, sometimes to cancer, but not cardiovascular disease, sometimes both, sometimes neither. Think about the retreat from fifty years of messaging about the dire threats to health of saturated fats and cholesterol.[9]

Disease associations need to be told in no uncertain terms that the primary causes of most of these chronic diseases can be traced to the SDoH. Even in cases in which the SDoH are not the primary cause of disease, such as with genetically determined diseases — Huntington's chorea and muscular dystrophy are two examples — the SDoH profoundly shape the lives of those so afflicted.

When experiencing the presence of a life-threatening or disabling disease — regardless of the causes — Canadian individuals and families are increasingly faced with health and social services of deteriorating quality, a lack of financial supports and increasing difficulty in achieving secure and well-paying employment, among other problems. At the very minimum, disease associations should recognize that deteriorating social conditions cause great harm to families facing the illnesses around which these organizations are organized.

The implications are obvious: disease associations that have influence with governments, policy-makers and the public — and are rich with resources — must join in advancing the SDoH agenda. Why have these organizations not taken action? The most benign explanation is that, like Canadians in general, they have been so subjected to lifestyle messages that they honestly do not know about the SDoH. Another explanation may be that, while they know about the SDoH being the primary causes of the diseases they pledge to eliminate, they worry that raising these issues will alienate their corporate sponsors and public donors. Why go out on a limb to raise issues that may threaten the agency when governments seem unlikely to act upon these issues anyway?

An even more dark reason may be that their boards of directors consist primarily of men and women from the corporate and business sector whose world-views are profoundly contradictory to a SDoH perspective. Consider that the chair of the board of the Heart and Stroke Foundation of Canada serves on the boards of numerous major equity corporations and the vice-chair is a managing director of a major private equity firm. Considering that these chronic diseases — especially heart disease and stroke — disproportionately afflict the poor and insecure, members of these boards should include all Canadians, not just the wealthy and secure. If there is any hope of seriously promoting the health of Canadians, these disease associations, like public health units across Canada, must become strong advocates for the SDoH approach. A good beginning would be diversifying these boards of directors to include members of Canadian society that do not come from the wealthiest 1 percent of the population.[10]

THE MEDIA

The media's coverage of health issues is narrow. Most often the focus is upon health care (for example, wait times, viral pandemics), biomedical research (isolation of disease genes, disease treatments) and health-related behaviours (diet, physical activity and tobacco and alcohol use). Canada is not alone in this trend: Australia, the Netherlands and the United Kingdom also experience narrow media coverage of health issues. An extensive analysis of media stories in major Canadian newspapers over an eight-year period shows this myopia. Of 4,732 newspaper articles concerned with health topics, there was a virtual blackout of stories concerned with the SDoH. Only 282 newspaper stories — 6 percent — were concerned with the socio-economic environment. More specifically, only nine stories (well below 1 percent) were concerned with how income — the primary social determinant of health — is related to health. There is no reason to think that radio and television coverage is any different.[11]

What Canadian newspaper health reporters say about how they went about reporting health stories reveals a similar bias. Most health reporters have just a rudimentary understanding of the SDoH and are far from convinced that the SDoH represented a topic worth reporting. The reasons given by reporters include lack of knowledge of the social determinants; difficulty putting the social determinants into the immediate and concrete "storytelling" that makes up typical news reporting; a perception that the social determinants are not new and therefore not newsworthy; and concern about stigmatizing the poor: "I guess what I'm saying is that the reporter may be worried about unfairly stigmatizing a certain income group, and unless and until you know that that income group is, you know, sicker than the rest of us, you may not want to have it out there."[12]

I would add that most media outlets — including newspapers — are owned by large corporate entities whose ideologies and values are not consistent with a SDoH perspective. Reporters are probably well aware of this, and like most other salaried workers, they hesitate to put their personal future on the line by consistently presenting a SDoH perspective in their stories.[13]

Clearly, there needs to be a systematic effort to shift how the Canadian media cover health issues. Citizens have an important role to play by writing letters to editors, health reporters and columnists about the narrow health reporting, demanding communication of the ever-expanding SDoH research to their readers. But the public cannot accomplish this alone. Public health agencies, disease associations, professional health associations such as the Canadian

Medical Association, Canadian Nurses Association and Canadian Public Health Association, and others concerned with promoting health must bring concerted and consistent pressure to bear upon the media to bring about a sea change in reporting. Another means of communicating the SDoH message may be through alternative media. The SDoH Listserv, an online discussion group run out of York University, provides a forum for over 1,200 members concerned with these issues. It has been operating since 2004 and plays an important role in dissemination of knowledge and ideas for action.[14]

MOBILIZING CANADIANS

Canadians can use knowledge about the SDoH to force the development and implementation of public policies to address the SDoH and their related health outcomes. Clearly, to date, Canadian governments have not been put under much pressure to take such actions. How can we change this?

Answering this question requires thinking about how Canadians can have their concerns met by agencies, institutions, governments and policy-makers. In a democratic society, responsiveness to citizen concerns is to be expected. But as the public policies that shape health have made distribution of economic and social resources more inequitable in Canada, many societal institutions have become less responsive to citizen concerns.[15]

Modern developed nations have characteristic ways of addressing public policy issues that are rooted in how their economic and political systems are organized. Why is it that the Nordic nations have public health and public policy approaches that focus on the SDoH, while Canada, the U.S. and the United Kingdom do rather less in this regard? The answer may lie in what has been termed the "worlds of welfare" view of public policy.

WORLDS OF WELFARE AND THE SDOH

Danish sociologist Gosta Esping-Andersen identifies three forms the welfare state in advanced wealthy nations. Canada, Australia, the U.S., the U.K. and Ireland constitute a cluster of nations called "liberal welfare states."[16] As shown in Chapter 2, liberal welfare states provide the least support and security to their citizens and show the worst health profiles in terms of life expectancy and infant mortality rates. Canada's public policy profile is closer to that of the U.S. and the U.K. than to European nations, where citizen security and support are more ensured.

Given the liberal disposition to minimize government's role in improving economic and social life, it is clear we need to shift how Canadians think about the role of the state and the market. Canadians understand that having the state deliver health care and public education is the most effective way to do this. Canadians also see a role for government in providing child-care and pharmacare but are less likely to view its role as providing post-secondary education, employment security and living wages. We should. The experiences of other nations show that the state is in the best position to improve the quality and equitable distribution of the SDoH. We therefore need a change in political culture in Canada.

In terms of many SDoH, for example income and housing, we know that there are many things that work and require significant investment by governments. But what is lacking is the political will to do them. To promote these shifts will require the support of the labour movement and political parties of the left. David Brady outlines the components of a strategy towards making such a shift: build citizen coalitions, shift the values and ideology of the public and strengthen political parties of the left and ensure their achieving power.[17]

BUILD CITIZEN COALITIONS

Canada has numerous groups whose purpose is to lobby governments and policy-makers to introduce progressive public policies. In these efforts, the groups also influence public opinion by educating Canadians about our political culture. Many of these groups focus directly or indirectly on the SDoH. These organizations connect Canadians with the latest information about social justice issues through newsletters and reports. Some organizations support progressive public policy in general. These organizations in essence deal with a wide range of social determinants. Others are focused on a specific SDoH (see Appendix). Canadians with knowledge of the SDoH and a commitment to organizing around this issue can join and/or support these groups.

The Canadian Centre for Policy Alternatives (CCPA) works on a wide range of public policy issues and has a strong affinity to the SDoH approach. It publishes the monthly CCPA *Monitor* and research reports on issues such as pensions, income inequality and poverty, housing and health care, among other topics. Its Living Wage project has developed a template for calculating the living wage in Canadian communities. The project encourages people who use the calculator to let them know what they come up with as they're working on keeping track of amounts across Canada.

The Social Research Planning Council, a Division of United Way Perth-Huron, collaborated with the CCPA-ON to produce a report detailing the living wage calculations for the Perth-Huron region of Ontario. This report built on the previous living wage work published by the CCPA and the Canadian Living Wage Framework, and used their calculator to determine a living wage of $16.47 per hour for Perth and Huron in 2015 for two adults working full-time with two children.[18]

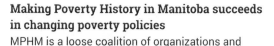

Making Poverty History in Manitoba succeeds in changing poverty policies

MPHM is a loose coalition of organizations and people in Manitoba promoting a comprehensive anti-poverty strategy. They produced a report, *The View from Here: Manitobans Call for a Poverty Reduction Program*, through a community research process. They sought and received endorsements from seventy organizations in Manitoba. They made sure that key provincial policy-makers knew about the process. In 2009, the provincial government responded with All Aboard: Manitoba's Poverty Reduction and Social Inclusion Strategy, and in 2012 with the Poverty Reduction Strategy Act. The Act included twenty-one indicators of poverty reduction and social inclusion along with targets and timelines for achieving them. Example are 3000 units of social housing in 2009–14, and increasing social assistance shelter benefits to 75 percent of market rent for 2014–18. The 75 percent shelter target was endorsed by 145 organizations in the province, who engaged in meetings with government officials, letter writing campaigns, provincial budget consultations, rallies at the legislature and engaging with local media.

Source: K. Bernas and S. MacKinnon, 2015, "Public Policy Advocacy and the Social Determinants of Health," in L. Fernandez, S. MacKinnon and J. Silver, The Social Determinants of Health in Manitoba, CCPA-Manitoba.

Anti-poverty groups such as Campaign 2000 and Canada without Poverty deal with public policy issues of income and its distribution, food security, housing and child-care. Many organizations focus on a specific social determinant of health, such as food security, housing, child-care or health care. Others focus on a specific health-related issue, such as poverty among Canadians of colour, women with disabilities, women's health or delivering health care to especially vulnerable Canadians. All of these organizations deserve the support of Canadians. They are means of getting governments and policy-makers to respond to our concerns.

SHIFT THE VALUES AND IDEOLOGY OF THE PUBLIC

Canadians opted for the development of medicare when they recognized that the capitalist economy was incapable of developing a universally accessible health care system. This quasi-socialist commitment to health care — as well as to elementary and secondary education — does not occur for other SDoH, such as guaranteed employment, provision of living wages and employment benefits or housing and food security, among others.

This can be attributed to the ongoing success of the corporate and business sector in advancing economic merit — that the economic system gives people what they deserve — as opposed to social justice — that everyone deserves to have their fundamental needs met — being the criterion for distributing economic and social resources. Most Canadians would clearly benefit from governments applying a social justice approach to public policy. And research indicates that Canadians are receptive to social justice arguments.[18] The problem is that they rarely hear these issues related to health by public health authorities, elected representatives and the media. This has to change.

ELECTORAL TACTICS

Every Canadian has elected representatives at the municipal, provincial/territorial and federal level. These individuals develop public policy that should be responsive to Canadians' needs. Almost every day these various levels of government address issues related to the SDoH. Even when a government is not responsible for an issue, it can lobby other government levels to enact policies or programs. For

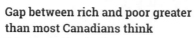

Gap between rich and poor greater than most Canadians think

Canadians drastically underestimate the country's wealth gap but still show broad support for policies such as higher income taxes to address the problem, according to new research by an Ottawa-based think tank.

"This is the first time this question has been looked at in Canada, namely people's perception of the wealth gap versus the reality," the Broadbent Institute's executive director, Rich Smith, told the Star.

"There's a huge discrepancy between the kind of Canada that people want and the kind of Canada that actually exists."

The research showed a strong appetite for government intervention to alleviate income inequality, with over 85 per cent of the country agreeing that the wealth gap was a problem.

Canadians agreed on specific measures to address inequality, too. Eighty per cent of those polled by the Institute supported higher federal income tax rates for the richest Canadians. Almost the same proportion were in favour of introducing higher corporate taxes.

Source: Sara Mojtehedzadeh, 2014, "Gap between rich and poor greater than most Canadians think," Toronto Star, December 16 <thestar.com/news/gta/2014/12/16/gap_between_rich_and_poor_greater_than_most_canadians_think.html>.

example, cities can lobby provincial governments to enact legislation that improves employment security and working conditions.

Identify your elected representative at each level and examine their personal position — as well as the party's position — on issues related to the SDoH. It may very well be that these people will not see the questions raised as being health issues. If that is the case, direct their attention to the available material about the SDoH and indicate that your future support will depend on the policy position taken.

POLITICAL PARTIES

There are numerous reasons why anyone truly concerned about the SDoH should engage with Canada's political parties. The first is that every political party puts forth policy positions that revolve around those pertinent questions. While there is ongoing concern about the failure of political parties to follow through on many of their campaign promises once they achieve power, a party's statement does at least provide insight about what *might* be expected in the form of public policy if the party gains power. And if the party does not follow through, it can be held to account in the next election.

The second reason for engaging with political parties is that clear evidence is emerging that wealthy industrialized nations ruled by social-democratic parties of the left — and also to some extent conservative parties that are truly progressive and not of the current North American variety — are more likely to produce public policy that strengthens the quality of the SDoH. This is especially the case in the Nordic nations.

PROFESSIONAL ORGANIZATIONS, EMPLOYEE ASSOCIATIONS AND UNIONS

Many Canadians belong to employment-related groups, such as unions and professional associations, and employer associations, such as school boards, children's aid societies and others. These associations have the means and the ability to issue statements and calls for governments to address issues related to the SDoH. Some of these associations have a specific affinity to the perspective if their members are physicians, nurses, psychologists, educators, public health workers, social workers, municipal service employees, immigration workers and early childhood education and care workers, among others. But all employment associations should be

Unions are good for your health

Karen White's just like you. She works in client care for Bell Aliant, which she has done for over six years. But unlike the Bell Mobility Call Centre in Mississauga, Karen's workplace is unionized.

"There are so many benefits of having a union, I don't know where to start," says the 31-year-old from Newfoundland. "We get pay progressions every six months until we reach the top of our wage scale, as well as negotiated annual increases. They are all the same, everyone gets them and the manager doesn't get to play favourites."

The pay is just the tip of the iceberg. "If I'm sick, I still get paid, day, evening and weekend shift work has to be shared evenly amongst all employees, a regular (or permanent) worker can't be laid off if our work is outsourced, and schedules have to be posted four weeks in advance," she explains. "The last one offers real 'work–life balance,' to borrow one of Bell's terms."

When it comes to career advancement, White says she has access to all the positions that come open.

"If I wanted to apply for an open job, I know that the company has to decide who to hire based on qualifications and seniority," she explains. "There are rules, the process is transparent and fair, and the managers are held accountable for the hiring decisions they make."

Source: MobilityUnion, 2010, "A Union Can Make a Difference in Your Life,' Says Nfld Bell Aliant Worker" <tinyurl.com/yetefwk>.

concerned with the SDoH as they affect the health and quality of life of all Canadians.

CHANGING HOW CANADA IS RUN

In recent years, Canada's institutions have become increasingly unresponsive to the needs of Canadians. The incomes of most Canadians are stagnating and employment is increasingly insecure. Social assistance and disability benefits lag behind inflation rates, pushing the most disadvantaged into even deeper conditions of deprivation. Food and housing insecurity are increasing. Social exclusion among vulnerable groups is growing.

The economic system denies access for many Canadians to the living and working conditions necessary for proper health. Governments are failing to address this state of affairs. The people responsible for this situation must be held accountable. The counterbalances — labour unions, citizen groups, civil society organizations and others — must be strengthened.

We have to engage and oppose those whose ideologies and values would turn Canada from a society with a market-based economy to a market-driven society.[19] We can look to our neighbour to the south to see what the costs of a market-driven society are to health.

Canadians must come to understand that the determinants of health and illness are primarily political, economic and social issues — not medical conditions or lifestyle choices. The distribution of health and illness is intimately tied up with how a society is organized and run. Health inequities result from social inequities. As Canadians come to understand this, the likelihood of governments and policymakers enacting public policies to promote health and prevent disease will increase. In the end, we just need the political will to improve the social determinants of health. This book is a call to action to shift us towards that crucial goal.

NOTES

Chapter 1: Who Stays Healthy? Who Gets Sick?

1. World Health Organization (WHO), 2008, *Closing the Gap in a Generation: Health Equity through Action on the Social Determinants of Health.*

2. Interviewed in *Unnatural Causes: Is Inequality Making Us Sick?* 2008, California Newsreel <unnaturalcauses.org/>.

3. J. Mikkonen and D. Raphael, 2010, *Social Determinants of Health: The Canadian Facts* <thecanadianfacts.org>.

4. Health Council of Canada, 2010, *Stepping It Up: Moving the Focus from Health Care in Canada to a Healthier Canada,* Health Council of Canada <healthcouncilcanada.ca/rpt_det.php?id=162>; see also Senate of Canada, 2009, *Health Disparities: Unacceptable for a Wealthy Country such as Canada* <//tinyurl.com/ye9erpo>.

5. D. Raphael (ed.), 2012, *Tackling Inequalities in Health: Lessons from International Experiences,* Canadian Scholars' Press.

6. L. Pal, 2006, *Beyond Policy Analysis: Public Issue Management in Turbulent Times,* Nelson Publishing.

7. H. Lasswell, 2011 [1936], *Politics: Who Gets What, When, How,* Literary Licensing, LLC; R. Labonte, 1993, *Health Promotion and Empowerment: Practice Frameworks,* Centre for Health Promotion and ParticipAction.

8. P. Townsend, N. Davidson and M. Whitehead (eds.), 1992, *Inequalities in Health: The Black Report and the Health Divide*, Penguin; D. Acheson, 1998, *Independent Inquiry into Inequalities in Health*, UK Stationary Office; M. Marmot et al., 2010, *Fair Society, Healthy Lives: The Marmot Review*, UCL Institute of Health Equity.

9. L. Lalonde, 1974, *A New Perspective on the Health of Canadians: A Working Document*, Health and Welfare Canada; J. Epp, 1986, *Achieving Health for All: A Framework for Health Promotion*, Health and Welfare Canada.

10. Canadian Public Health Association, 1996, *Action Statement for Health Promotion in Canada* <cpha.ca/en/programs/policy/action.aspx>; A. Manzano and D. Raphael, 2010, "CPHA and the Social Determinants of Health: An Analysis of Policy Documents and Recommendations for Future Action," *Canadian Journal of Public Health* 101 (5); Senate reports are available at <//tinyurl.com/2zqg9o and //tinyurl.com/np4btx>.

11. World Health Organization (WHO), 2008, *Closing the Gap*.

12. Statistics Canada, 2016, *Table 102-0122: Health-adjusted life expectancy, at birth and at age 65, by sex and income, Canada and provinces, 2005–2007* <statcan.gc.ca/cansim/a26?lang=eng&id=1020122&p2=46>.

13. Canadian Institute for Health Information (CIHI), 2009, *Too Early, Too Small: A Profile of Small Babies across Canada*.

14. Canadian Institute for Health Information, CIHI, 2010, *Injury Hospitalizations and Socio-Economic Status* <secure.cihi.ca/free_products/Injury_aib_vE4CCF_v3_en.pdf>.

15. G. Davey Smith et al., 2005, "Genetic Epidemiology and Public Health: Hope, Hype, and Future Prospects," *Lancet* 366.

16. S. Nettleton, 1997, "Surveillance, Health Promotion and the Formation of a Risk Identity," in M. Sidell, L. Jones, J. Katz and A. Peberdy (eds.), *Debates and Dilemmas in Promoting Health*. Open University Press; Canadian Population Health Initiative (CPHI), 2004, *Select Highlights on Public Views of the Determinants of Health*.

17. G. Xi, 2005, "Income Inequality and Health in Ontario," *Canadian*

Journal of Public Health 96.

18. M. Shields and S. Tremblay, 2002, "The Health of Canada's Communities," *Health Reports Supplement* 13 (July).

19. G. Davey Smith (ed.), 2003, *Inequalities in Health: Life Course Perspectives,* Policy Press.

20. M. Gasher et al., 2007. "Spreading the News: Social Determinants of Health Reportage in Canadian Daily Newspapers," *Canadian Journal of Communication* 32 (3): 557–574; M. Hayes et al., 2007, "Telling Stories: News Media, Health Literacy and Public Policy in Canada," *Social Science and Medicine* 54.

21. J. McKinlay and S.M. McKinlay, 1987, "Medical Measures and the Decline of Mortality," in H.D. Schwartz (ed.), *Dominant Issues in Medical Sociology,* second edition, Random House.

22. T. McKeown, 1976, *The Role of Medicine: Dream, Mirage, or Nemesis,* Neufeld Provincial Hospitals Trust; T. McKeown and R.G. Record, 1975, "An Interpretation of the Decline in Mortality in England and Wales during the Twentieth Century," *Population Studies* 29.

23. G. Olsen, 2002, *The Politics of the Welfare State,* Oxford University Press.

24. D. Kuh, Y, Ben Shlomo and E. Susser (eds.), 2004, *A Life Course Approach to Chronic Disease Epidemiology,* second edition, Oxford University Press.

25. G. Scambler, 2002, *Health and Social Change: A Critical Theory.* Open University Press; C. Leys, 2001, *Market-Driven Politics,* Verso.

Chapter 2: Living Conditions, Stress and the Human Body

1. Statistics Canada, 2014, *Perceived Life Stress, 2014* <statcan.gc.ca/pub/82-625-x/2015001/article/14188-eng.htm>.

2. E. Brunner and M.G. Marmot, 2006, "Social Organization, Stress, and Health," in M.G. Marmot and R.G. Wilkinson (eds.), *Social Determinants of Health,* second edition, Oxford University Press.

3. P. Martikainen, M. Bartley, and E. Lahelma, 2002, "Psychosocial Determinants of Health in Social Epidemiology," *International Journal*

of Epidemiology 31 (6).

4. B. Lindström and M. Eriksson, 2006, "Contextualizing Salutogenesis and Antonovsky in Public Health Development," *Health Promotion International* 21 (3).

5. M. Benzeval et al., 2001, "Income and Health over the Lifecourse: Evidence and Policy Implications," in H. Graham (ed.), *Understanding Health Inequalities,* Open University Press.

6. S. Lupien et al., 2001, "Can Poverty Get under Your Skin? Basal Cortisol Levels and Cognitive Function in Children from Low and High Socioeconomic Status," *Development and Psychopathology,* 13; D. Raphael, 2010, "The Lived Experience of Poverty," in D. Raphael (ed.), *Poverty in Canada: Implications for Health and Quality of Life,* Canadian Scholars' Press; G. Davey Smith, Y. Ben-Shlomo, and J. Lynch, 2002, "Life Course Approaches to Inequalities in Coronary Heart Disease Risk," in S.A. Stansfeld and M. Marmot (eds.), *Stress and the Heart: Psychosocial Pathways to Coronary Heart Disease,* British Medical Journal Books.

7. L. Potvin, L. Richard, and A. Edwards, 2000, "Knowledge of Cardiovascular Disease Risk Factors among the Canadian Population: Relationships with Indicators of Socioeconomic Status," *Canadian Medical Association Journal* 162.

8. M. Shaw, D. Dorling, D. Gordon and G. Davey Smith, G., 1999, *The Widening Gap: Health Inequalities and Policy in Britain,* Policy Press.

9. M. Bartley, 2003, *Understanding Health Inequalities,* Polity Press.

10. C. Hertzman and C. Power, 2003, "Health and Human Development: Understandings from Life-Course Research," *Developmental Neuropsychology* 24 (2&3).

11. D. Barker, 2001, "Size at Birth and Resilience to Effects of Poor Living Conditions in Adult Life: Longitudinal Study," *British Medical Journal — Clinical Research* 323 (7324); P.T. James et al., 1997, "Socioeconomic Determinants of Health: The Contribution of Nutrition to Inequalities in Health," *British Medical Journal* 314 (7093).

12. J.D. Willms (ed.), 2002, *Vulnerable Children: Findings from Canada's*

National Longitudinal Survey, University of Alberta Press.

13. R.G. Wilkinson and S. Bezruchka, 2002, "Income Inequality and Population Health," *British Medical Journal* 324 (7343): 978; D. Raphael, 2011, "Canadian Public Policy and Poverty in International Perspective," in D. Raphael (ed.), *Poverty in Canada: Implications for Health and Quality of Life*, Canadian Scholars' Press; D. Raphael, 2014, "Social Determinants of Children's Health in Canada: Analysis and Implications," *International Journal of Child, Youth and Family Studies* 5 (2).

14. D. Coburn, 2000, "Income Inequality, Social Cohesion and the Health Status of Populations: The Role of Neo-Liberalism," *Social Science & Medicine* 51 (1).

15. T. Grant and J. McFarland, November 14, 2013, "How Globalization Has Left the 1 Per Cent Even Further Ahead," *Globe and Mail* <theglobeandmail.com/news/national/time-to-lead/how-globalization-has-left-the-1-per-cent-even-further-ahead/article15433419/?page=all>.

16. D. Coburn, 2004, "Beyond the Income Inequality Hypothesis: Globalization, Neo-Liberalism, and Health Inequalities," *Social Science & Medicine* 58.

17. F. Vandenbroucke, 2002, "Foreword," in G. Esping-Andersen (ed.), *Why We Need a New Welfare State*, Oxford University Press; D. Langille, 2016, "Follow the Money: How Business and Politics Shape Our Health," in D. Raphael (ed.), *Social Determinants of Health: Canadian Perspectives*, third edition, Canadian Scholars' Press; S. Saint-Arnaud and P. Bernard, 2003, "Convergence or Resilience? A Hierarchal Cluster Analysis of the Welfare Regimes in Advanced Countries," *Current Sociology* 51 (5).

18. V. Navarro and L. Shi, 2002, "The Political Context of Social Inequalities and Health," In V. Navarro (ed.), *The Political Economy of Social Inequalities: Consequences for Health and Quality of Life*, Baywood.

19. M-F. Raynault, D. Côté, and S. Chartrand, 2015, *Scandinavian Common Sense: Policies to Tackle Social Inequalities in Health*, Baraka

Books.

20. C. Bambra, 2007, "Going Beyond the Three Worlds of Welfare Capitalism: Regime Theory and Public Health Research," *Journal of Epidemiology and Community Health* 61 (12).

Chapter 3: Income, Education and Work

1. Public Health Agency of Canada, 2013, *What Makes Canadians Healthy or Unhealthy?* <http://www.phac-aspc.gc.ca/ph-sp/ determinants/determinants-eng.php>.

2. T. Bryant, 2016, "Implications of Public Policy Change Models for Addressing Income-Related Health Inequalities," *Canadian Public Policy,* 41 (Supplement 2): S10-S16.

3. G. Menahem, 2010, *How Can the Decommodified Security Ratio Assess Social Protection Systems?* LIS Working Paper No. 529, Luxembourg Income Study <www.ief.es/documentos/recursos/publicaciones/ papeles_trabajo/2008_11.pdf>; M. Shaw et al., 1999, *The Widening Gap: Health Inequalities and Policy in Britain,* Policy Press.

4. M. Stewart, et al., 2008, "Left Out: Perspectives on Social Exclusion and Inclusion Across Income Groups," *Health Sociology Review* 17: 78–94.

5. N. Auger and C. Alix, 2016, "Income, Income Distribution, and Health in Canada," in D. Raphael (ed.), *Social Determinants of Health: Canadian Perspectives,* third edition, Canadian Scholars' Press.

6. M. Lemstra, M. Rogers and J. Moraros, 2015, "Income and Heart Disease: Neglected Risk Factor," *Canadian Family Physician* 61 (12): 698–704.

7. S. Dinca-Panaitescua et al., 2011, "Diabetes Prevalence and income: Results of the Canadian Community Health Survey," *Health Policy* 99: 116–123; S. Dinca-Panaitescua et al., 2012, "The Dynamics of the Relationship Between the Experience of Low Income and Type 2 Diabetes: Longitudinal Results," *Maturitas* 72: 229–235.

8. D. McKeown et al., 2008, *The Unequal City: Income and Health Inequalities in Toronto,* Toronto Public Health; D. Barker et al., 2001,

"Size at Birth and Resilience to Effects of Poor Living Conditions in Adult Life: Longitudinal Study," *British Medical Journal, Clinical Research* 323 (7324): 1273–1276; Innocenti Research Centre, 2001, *A League Table of Teenage Births in Rich Nations;* J.D. Willms, 1999, "Quality and Inequality in Children's Literacy: The Effects of Families, Schools and Communities," in D.P. Keating and C. Hertzman (eds.), *Developmental Health and the Wealth of Nations: Social, Biological and Educational Dynamics,* Guilford Press; Canadian Population Health Initiative (CPHI), 2008, *Reducing Gaps in Health: A Focus on Socio-Economic Status in Urban Canada.*

9. Organisation for Economic Co-operation and Development (OECD), 2008, *Growing Unequal: Income Distribution and Poverty in OECD Nations;* OECD. 2015, *In It Together: Why Less Inequality Benefits All.*

10. A. Curry-Stevens, 2009, "Precarious Changes: A Generational Exploration of Canadian Incomes and Wealth," in D. Raphael (ed.), *Social Determinants of Health: Canadian Perspectives,* third edition, Canadian Scholars' Press.

11. Canadian Population Health Initiative (CPHI), 2004, *Improving the Health of Canadians.*

12. D. Raphael, 2010, *Poverty in Canada: Implications for Health and Quality of Life,* second edition, Canadian Scholars' Press.

13. C. Ungerleider and T. Burns, 2016, "The State and Quality of Canadian Public Elementary and Secondary Education," In D. Raphael (ed.), *Social Determinants of Health: Canadian Perspectives,* third edition, Canadian Scholars' Press.

14. PISA Database <http://www.oecd.org/pisa/pisaproducts/>; Organisation for Economic Co-operation and Development (OECD), 2014, *PISA 2012 Results in Focus: What 15 Year Olds Know and What They Can Do with What They Know.*

15. B. Ronson McNichol and I. Rootman, 2016, "Literacy and Health Literacy: New Understandings about Their Impact on Health," in D. Raphael (ed.), *Social Determinants of Health: Canadian Perspectives,* third edition, Canadian Scholars' Press.

16. M. Bartley, 1994, "Unemployment and Ill Health: Understanding

the Relationship," *Journal of Epidemiology and Community Health* 48: 333–337.

17. D.G. Tremblay, 2009, "Precarious Work and the Labour Market," in D. Raphael (ed.), *Social Determinants of Health: Canadian Perspectives,* second edition, Canadian Scholars' Press.

18. E. Tompa, M. Polanyi, and J. Foley, 2016, "Labour Market Flexibility and Worker Insecurity," in D. Raphael (ed.), *Social Determinants of Health: Canadian Perspectives,* third edition, Canadian Scholars' Press.

19. W. Lewchuk et al., 2006, "The Hidden Costs of Precarious Employment: Health and the Employment Relationship," in L. Vosko (ed.), *Precarious Work in Canada,* McGill Queen's University Press; M. Bartley, 1994, "Unemployment and Ill Health: Understanding the Relationship," *Journal of Epidemiology and Community Health* 48: 333–337.

20. Tompa, Polanyi and Foley, 2016, "Labour Market Flexibility."

21. A. Jackson and G. Rao, 2016, "The Unhealthy Canadian Workplace," in D. Raphael (ed.), *Social Determinants of Health: Canadian Perspectives,* third edition, Canadian Scholars' Press.

22. P. Smith and M. Polanyi, 2016, "Understanding and Improving the Health of Work," in D. Raphael (ed.), *Social Determinants of Health: Canadian Perspectives,* third edition, Canadian Scholars' Press.

23. A. Jackson, 2010, *Work and Labour in Canada: Critical Issues,* second edition, Canadian Scholars' Press.

24. Jackson and Rao, 2016, "The Unhealthy Canadian Workplace."

25. Canadian Centre for Occupational Health and Safety, n.d., "April 28, National Day of Mourning" <ccohs.ca/events/mourning/>.

26. Jackson and Rao, 2016, "The Unhealthy Canadian Workplace."

27. This study was widely reported in a public-friendly format at <www.thinkupstream.net/health_effects_of_income_inequality> and <www.thestar.com/opinion/commentary/2014/11/23/income_inequality_is_killing_thousands_of_canadians_every_year.html>.

Chapter 4: Early Child Development,
Food Security and Housing

1. M. Friendly, 2016, "Early Childhood Education and Care as a Social Determinant of Health," in D. Raphael (ed.), *Social Determinants of Health: Canadian Perspectives,* second edition, Canadian Scholars' Press.

2. D. Raphael, 2016, "Early Child Development and Health," in D. Raphael (ed.), *Social Determinants of Health: Canadian Perspectives,* second edition, Canadian Scholars' Press; T. Bryant, 2016, "Housing and Health," in D. Raphael (ed.), *Social Determinants of Health: Canadian Perspectives,* third edition, Canadian Scholars' Press.

3. M. Rioux, 2010, "The Right to Health: Human Rights Approaches to Health," in T. Bryant, D. Raphael, and M. Rioux (eds.), *Staying Alive: Critical Perspectives on Health, Illness, and Health Care,* second edition, Canadian Scholars' Press; R. Miko and S. Thompson, 2004, "Pay the Rent or Feed the Kids? Tough Choices," *Women and Environments International Journal* 62 (63); CBC, May 16, 2012, *UN Official Sparks Debate over Canadian Food Security* <cbc.ca/news/politics/un-official-sparks-debate-over-canadian-food-security-1.1130281>; United Nations, November 1, 2007, *United Nations Expert on Adequate Housing Calls for Immediate Attention to Tackle National Housing Crisis in Canada* <ohchr.org/en/NewsEvents/Pages/DisplayNews.aspx?NewsID=4822&LangID=E>.

4. World Health Organization, 2015, *Early Child Development* <who.int/social_determinants/themes/earlychilddevelopment/en/>.

5. C. Hertzman and J. Frank, 2006, "Biological Pathways Linking the Social Environment, Development, and Health," in J. Heymann, C. Hertzman, M. Barer and R.G. Evans (eds.), *Healthier Societies: From Analysis to Action,* Oxford University Press.

6. J. Eriksson et al., 1999, "Catch-Up Growth in Childhood and Death from Coronary Heart Disease: Longitudinal Study," *British Medical Journal — Clinical Research* 318 (7181); A. Antonovsky, 1987, *Unraveling the Mystery of Health: How People Manage Stress and Stay*

Well, Jossey Bass; J. Lynch, G. Kaplan, and J. Salonen, 1997, "Why Do Poor People Behave Poorly? Variation in Adult Health Behaviours and Psychosocial Characteristics by Stages of the Socioeconomic Lifecourse," *Social Science and Medicine* 44 (6).

7. C. Hertzman, 2001, "Population Health and Child Development: A View From Canada," in J.A. Auerbach and B. Krimgold (eds.), *Income, Socioeconomic Status, and Health: Exploring the Relationships,* National Policy Association; J.D. Willms (ed.), 2002, *Vulnerable Children: Findings from Canada's National Longitudinal Survey,* University of Alberta Press.

8. J.D. Willms, 2003, "Literacy Proficiency of Youth: Evidence of Converging Socioeconomic Gradients," *International Journal of Educational Research* 39; D. Evans, C. Hertzman, and S. Morgan, 2007, "Improving Health Outcomes in Canada," in J. Leonard, C. Ragan, and F. St-Hilaire (eds.), *A Canadian Priorities Agenda: Policy Choices to Improve Economic and Social Well-Being,* Institute for Research on Public Policy.

9. Campaign 2000, 2015, *2014 Report Card on Child and Family Poverty in Canada* <campaign2000.ca/anniversaryreport/CanadaRC2014EN. pdf>; Organisation for Economic Cooperation and Development, 2016, *Families and Children* <oecd.org/els/family/>.

10. Innocenti Research Centre, 2008, *The Child Care Transition: A League Table of Early Childhood Education and Care in Economically Advanced Countries,* Report Card No. 6; Friendly, 2016, "Early Childhood Education and Care as a Social Determinant of Health."

11. L. McIntyre and L. Anderson, 2016, "Food Insecurity," in D. Raphael (ed.), *Social Determinants of Health: Canadian Perspectives*, third edition, Canadian Scholars' Press.

12. S.I. Kirkpatrick and V. Tarasuk, 2008, "Food Insecurity Is Associated with Nutrient Inadequacies among Canadian Adults and Adolescents," *Journal of Nutrition* 138 (3); V. Tarasuk, 2016, "Food Insecurity and Health," in D. Raphael (ed.), *Social Determinants of Health: Canadian Perspectives,* third edition, Canadian Scholars' Press.

13. N. Vozoris and V. Tarasuk, 2003, "Household Food Insufficiency Is

Associated with Poorer Health," *Journal of Nutrition* 133.

14. V. Tarasuk, 2009, "Food Insecurity and Health."

15. L. McIntyre and L. Anderson, 2016, "Food Insecurity."

16. V. Tarasuk, 2009, "Food Insecurity and Health."

17. Canadian Association of Food Banks, 2015, *Hungercount 2015: A Comprehensive Report on Hunger and Food Bank Use in Canada and Recommendations for Change.*

18. L. McIntyre and L. Anderson, 2016, "Food Insecurity."

19. L. McIntyre and L. Anderson, 2016, "Food Insecurity."

20. L. McIntyre and L. Anderson, 2016, "Food Insecurity."

21. World Health Organization, 1986, *Ottawa Charter for Health Promotion.*

22. T. Bryant and Michael Shapcott, 2016, "Housing," in D. Raphael (ed.), *Social Determinants of Health: Canadian Perspectives,* third edition, Canadian Scholars' Press; T. Bryant, D. Raphael, T. Schrecker, and R. Labonte, 2011, "Canada: A Land of Missed Opportunity for Addressing the Social Determinants of Health," *Health Policy* 101 (1).

23. J. Dunn, 2002, *A Population Health Approach to Housing: A Framework For Research,* National Housing Research Committee and CMHC.

24. T. Bryant, 2016,"Housing and Health"; S. Hwang et al., 1999, "Housing and Population Health: A Review of the Literature," Centre for Applied Social Research Faculty of Social Work, University of Toronto.

25. A. Savage, 1988, *Warmth in Winter: Evaluation of an Information Pack for Elderly People,* Cardiff University of Wales College of Medicine Research Team for the Care of the Elderly; D. Strachan, 1988, "Damp Housing and Childhood Asthma: Validation of Reporting of Symptoms," *British Medical Journal* 297; S. Platt, C. Martin, S. Hunt, and C. Lewis, 1989, "Damp Housing, Mould Growth and Symptomatic Health State," *British Medical Journal* 298.

26. T. Bryant, 2016, "Housing and Health"; A. Marsh, D. Gordon, C. Pantazis, and P. Heslop, 1999, *Home Sweet Home? The Impact of Poor Housing on Health,* Policy Press; D.J. Dedman et al., 2001, "Childhood Housing Conditions and Later Mortality in the Boyd Orr Cohort,"

Journal of Epidemiology and Community Health 55.

27. E. Ambrosio, D. Baker, C. Crowe and K. Hardill, 1992, *The Street Health Report: A Study of the Health Status and Barriers to Health Care of Homeless Women and Men in the City of Toronto,* Street Health.

28. C. Kushner, 1998, "Better Access, Better Care: A Research Paper on Health Services and Homelessness in Toronto," Toronto Mayor's Homelessness Action Task Force; S. Hwang, 2001, "Homelessness and Health," *Canadian Medical Association Journal* 164 (2); A. Cheung and S. Hwang, 2004, "Risk of Death among Homeless Women: A Cohort Study and Review of the Literature," *Canadian Medical Association Journal* 170 (8).

29. Canada Mortgage and Housing Corporation, 2009, "Housing in Canada On-line" <cmhc.beyond2020.com/>; D. Hulchanski, 2001, *A Tale of Two Canada's: Homeowners Getting Richer, Renters Getting Poorer,* Centre For Urban and Community Studies, University of Toronto; D. Hulchanski, 2010, *The Three Cities within Toronto: Income Polarization Among Toronto's Neighbourhoods, 1970–20050,* Centre for Urban and Community Studies, University of Toronto <urbancentre. utoronto.ca/pdfs/curp/tnrn/Three-Cities-Within-Toronto-2010-Final.pdf>.

30. Statistics Canada, 2004, "Owner Households and Tenant Households by Major Payments and Gross Rent as a Percentage of 1995 Household Income," 1996 Census, Census Metropolitan Areas; Federation of Canadian Municipalities, 2004, Income, Shelter and Necessities.

Chapter 5: Social Exclusion

1. G.E. Galabuzi, 2016, "Social Exclusion," in D. Raphael (ed.), *Social Determinants of Health: Canadian Perspectives,* third edition, Canadian Scholars' Press.

2. P. White, 1998, "Ideologies, Social Exclusion and Spatial Segregation in Paris," in S. Mursterd and W. Ostendorf (eds.), *Urban Degradation and the Welfare State: Inequality and Exclusion in Western Cities,*

Routledge; T. Wojtasiewicz, 2008, "Easing Barriers for Newcomer Physicians," *Canadian Newcomer Magazine* 20 (4).

3. Adapted from J. Smylie and M. Firestone, 2016, "The Health of Indigenous Peoples," in D. Raphael (ed.), *Social Determinants of Health: Canadian Perspectives,* third edition, Canadian Scholars' Press.

4. G.E. Galabuzi, 2016, "Social Exclusion."

5. J. Smylie and M. Firestone, 2016, "The Health of Indigenous Peoples."

6. G.E. Galabuzi, 2016, "Social Exclusion."

7. M. Ornstein, 2006, *Ethno-Racial Groups in Toronto, 1971–2001: A Demographic and Social-economic Profile*, City of Toronto.

8. G.E. Galabuzi, 2005, *Canada's Economic Apartheid: The Social Exclusion of Racialized Groups in the New Century,* Canadian Scholars' Press.

9. J. McMullin, 2009, *Understanding Social Inequality: Intersections of Class, Age, Gender, Ethnicity and Race in Canada,* second edition, Oxford University Press; I. Hyman, 2001, "Immigration and Health" <hc-sc.gc.ca/iacb-dgiac/arad draa/english/rmdd/wpapers/ Immigration.pdf>; E. Ng, R. Wilkins, F. Gendron, and J.M. Berthelot, 2005, *Healthy Today, Healthy Tomorrow? Findings from the National Population Health Survey,* Statistics Canada.

10. M. Wallis and S. Kwok (eds.), 2008, *Daily Struggles: The Deepening Racialization and Feminization of Poverty in Canada,* Canadian Scholars' Press; N. Ross, K. Nobrega, and J. Dunn, 2001, "Income Segregation, Income Inequality and Mortality in North American Metropolitan Areas," *GeoJournal* 53 (2): 117–124.

11. P. Armstrong, 2016, "Public Policy, Gender, and Health," in D. Raphael (ed.), *Social Determinants of Health: Canadian Perspectives,* third edition, Canadian Scholars' Press.

12. Statistics Canada, 2015, "Table 282-0073," *Labour Force Survey Estimates, Wages of Employees,* Statistics Canada <statcan.gc.ca/ cansim/a26?lang=eng&id=2820073>; M. Drolet, 2001, *The Persistent Gap: New Evidence on the Canadian Gender Wage Cap,* Analytic Studies Branch, Statistics Canada.

13. A. Curry-Stevens, 2009, "When Economic Growth Doesn't Trickle

Down: The Wage Dimensions of Income Polarization," in D. Raphael (ed.), *Social Determinants of Health: Canadian Perspectives,* second edition, Canadian Scholars' Press.

14. Statistics Canada, 2016, "Life Expectancy, at Birth and at Age 65, by Sex and by Province and Territory" <statcan.gc.ca/tables-tableaux/ sum-som/l01/cst01/health72a-eng.htm>; M. DesMeules, L. Turner, and R. Cho, 2003, "Morbidity Experiences and Disability among Canadian Women," in M. DesMeules et al. (eds.), *Women's Health Surveillance Report: A Multi-dimensional Look at the Health of Canadian Women,* Health Canada, Canadian Population Health Initiative; M.T. Ruiz and L.M. Verbrugge, 1997, "A Two-Way View of Gender Bias in Medicine," *Journal of Epidemiology and Community Health* 51; F. Trovato and N.M. Lalu, 1996, "Narrowing Sex Differentials in Life Expectancy in the Industrialized World: Early 1970s to Early 1990s," *Social Biology* 43 (1–2).

15. Statistics Canada, 2015, "A Profile of Persons with Disabilities among Canadians Aged 15 Years or Older, 2012" <http://www.statcan.gc.ca/ pub/89-654-x/89-654-x2015001-eng.htm#a4>.

16. Organisation for Economic Co-operation and Development (OECD), 2015, *Social Expenditure Database* <http://stats.oecd.org/Index. aspx?datasetcode=SOCX_AGG>.

17. Canadian Council on Social Development, 2005, *Employment and Persons with Disabilities in Canada.* The quotation "Employers are still ignorant…" is from Canadian Abilities Foundation, 2004, "Neglected or Hidden," Toronto: p. 9.

Chapter 6: Public Policy and the Social Determinants of Health

1. Canadian Public Health Association, 1996, *Action Statement for Health Promotion in Canada* <http://www.cpha.ca/en/programs/policy/ action.aspx>.

2. World Health Organization, 2008, *Closing the Gap in a Generation: Health Equity Through Action on the Social Determinants of Health,* p. 1.

3. Commission on Social Determinants of Health, May 2005, *Towards a Framework for Analysis and Action on the Social Determinants of Health*, Discussion Paper, WHO Health Equity Team <www.determinants. fiocruz.br/pdf/texto/In_texto2.pdf>.

4. Pierre Fortin, Luc Godbout and Suzie St-Cerny, 2015, "Impact of Quebec's Universal Low-Fee Childcare Program on Female Labour force Participation, Domestic Income and Government," University of Toronto <oise.utoronto.ca/atkinson/UserFiles/File/News/Fortin-Godbout-St_Cerny_eng.pdf.>.

5. M-F. Raynault, D. Côté, and S. Chartrand, 2015, *Scandinavian Common Sense: Policies to Tackle Social Inequalities in Health,* Baraka Books.

6. J. Mikkonen and D. Raphael, 2010, *Social Determinants of Health: The Canadian Facts* <http://thecanadianfasct.org>; S. Saint-Arnaud and P. Bernard, 2003, "Convergence or Resilience? A Hierarchical Cluster Analysis of the Welfare Regimes in Advanced Countries," *Current Sociology* 51 (5): 499–527.

7. M. Shaw, D. Dorling, D. Gordon, and G.D. Smith, 1999, *The Widening Gap: Health Inequalities and Policy in Britain,* Policy Press.

8. G. Esping-Andersen, 2002, "A Child-Centred Social Investment Strategy," in G. Esping-Andersen (ed.), *Why We Need a New Welfare State,* Oxford University Press, p. 19.

9. Organisation for Economic Cooperation and Development (OECD), 2016, *Level of GDP Per Capita and Productivity* <stats.oecd.org/Index. aspx?DataSetCode=PDB_LV>.

10. Organisation for Economic Cooperation and Development (OECD), 2015, *Health at a Glance 2015, OECD Indicators*; Robert Wood Johnson Foundation, 2008, *Overcoming Obstacles to Health,* Princeton: Robert Wood Johnson Foundation.

11. Organisation for Economic Cooperation and Development (OECD), 2016, *Social Expenditure Database (SOCX)* <http://www.oecd.org/ social/expenditure.htm>.

12. Organisation for Economic Cooperation and Development (OECD), 2015, *Society at a Glance, 2015 Indicators.*

13. Innocenti Research Centre, 2005, *Child Poverty in Rich Nations, Report Card No. 6*; T. Smeeding, 2005, "Poor People in Rich Nations: The United States in Comparative Perspective," Luxembourg Income Study Working Paper #419, Syracuse University.

14. Organisation for Economic Cooperation and Development (OECD), 2016, *Earnings and Wages* <https://data.oecd.org/earnwage/wage-levels.htm>.

15. D. Raphael, 2009, "Reducing Social and Health Inequalities Requires Building Social and Political Movements," *Humanity and Society* 33, (1/2): 145–165.

16. M. Lee, 2007, *Eroding Tax Fairness: Tax Incidence in Canada, 1998 to 2005*, Canadian Centre for Policy Alternatives.

17. Organisation for Economic Cooperation and Development (OECD), 2016, *Unemployment Rate* <https://data.oecd.org/unemp/unemployment-rate.htm>; Organisation for Economic Cooperation and Development (OECD), 2016, *Employment Protection* <http://stats.oecd.org/Index.aspx?DataSetCode=EPL_OV>.

18. Organisation for Economic Cooperation and Development (OECD), 2016, "Social Expenditure Database (SOCX)" <http://www.oecd.org/social/expenditure.htm>.

19. E. Tompa, M. Polanyi and J. Foley, 2016, "Labour Market Flexibility and Worker Insecurity," in D. Raphael (ed.), *Social Determinants of Health: Canadian Perspectives*, third edition, Canadian Scholars' Press.

20. A. Jackson and G. Rao, 2016, "The Unhealthy Canadian Workplace," in D. Raphael (ed.), *Social Determinants of Health: Canadian Perspectives*, third edition, Canadian Scholars' Press.

21. E. Tompa, M. Polanyi and J. Foley, 2016, "Labour Market Flexibility and Worker Insecurity."

22. Organisation for Economic Cooperation and Development (OECD), 2013, *Economic Policy Reform 2013*.

23. Government of Canada, 1994, *Report of the Advisory Group on Working Time and the Distribution of Work*, Human Resources and Development Canada; Canada, 1997, *Report of the Collective Reflection on the Changing Workplace*, Human Resources and Development

Canada; Human Resources and Skills Development Canada (HRSD), 2006, *Fairness at Work: Federal Labour Standards for the 21st Century*.

24. E. Tompa, M. Polanyi and J. Foley, 2016, "Labour Market Flexibility and Worker Insecurity."

25. A. Jackson and G. Rao, 2016, "The Unhealthy Canadian Workplace."

26. Organisation for Economic Cooperation and Development (OECD), 2016, *Earnings and Wages* <https://data.oecd.org/earnwage/wage-levels.htm>.

27. Organisation for Economic Cooperation and Development (OECD), 2015, *Education at a Glance* <http://www.oecd.org/edu/education-at-a-glance-19991487.htm>.

28. B. McNichol and I. Rootman, 2016, "Literacy and Health Literacy: New Understandings about Their Impact on Health," in D. Raphael (ed.), *Social Determinants of Health: Canadian Perspectives,* third edition, Canadian Scholars' Press.

29. J. Silver, 2013, *Moving Forward, Giving Back: Transformative Aboriginal Adult Education*, Fernwood Publishing, p. 13.

30. J. Beach et al., 2009, *Early Childhood Education and Care in Canada 2008,* Childcare Resource and Research Unit; Organisation for Economic Co-operation and Development (OECD), 2009 <www.oecd.org/dataoecd/44/20/38954032.xls>.

31. D. Raphael, 2014, "Social Determinants of Children's Health in Canada: Analysis and Implications," *International Journal of Child, Youth and Family Studies* 5 (2): 220–239.

32. D. Raphael, 2014, "Social Determinants of Children's Health in Canada: Analysis and Implications."

33. D. Langille, 2009, "Follow the Money: How Business and Politics Shape Our Health," in D. Raphael, (ed.), *Social Determinants of Health: Canadian Perspectives*, third edition, Canadian Scholars' Press; Newfoundland and Labrador Business Coalition, 2008, *Submission to the 2008 Minimum Wage Review: Impacts on Business*.

34. Innocenti Research Centre, 2005,*Child Poverty in Rich Nations, 2005. Report Card No. 6*.

35. J. Temple, 2008, "Severe and Moderate Forms of Food Insecurity: Are

They Distinguishable?" *Australian Journal of Social Issues* 43: 649–668; M. Nord and H.A. Hopwood, 2008, *Comparison of Household Food Security in Canada and the United States,* U.S. Dept. of Agriculture; C. McKerchar, 2006, "Food Security in New Zealand: A Very Brief Overview" <www.ana.org.nz/documents/ChristinaMcKerchar.pdf>.

36. L. McIntyre and L. Anderson, 2016, "Food Insecurity," in D. Raphael (ed.), *Social Determinants of Health: Canadian Perspectives,* third edition, TCanadian Scholars' Press.

37. N. Wiebe and K. Wipf, 2011, "Nurturing Food Sovereignty in Canada," in H. Wittman, A. Desmarais and N. Wiebe (eds), *Food Sovereignty in Canada,* Fernwood Publishing; E. Smirl, 2015, "Shifting the Tables," in L. Fernandez, S. MacKinnon and J. Silver (eds.), *The Social Determinants of Health in Manitoba.* CCPA-Manitoba.

38. Organisation for Economic Cooperation and Development (OECD), 2016, *Public Spending on Housing* <https://stats.oecd.org/Index. aspx?DataSetCode=SOCX_AGG>; I.Skelton, 2015, "Privatizing a Social Need," in J. Brandon and J. Silver (eds.), *Poor Housing,* Fernwood Publishing.

39. Federation of Canadian Municipalities (FCM), 2015, *Built to Last: Strengthening the Foundations of Housing in Canada,* FCM.

40. I. Skelton, "Privatizing a Social Need."

41. M. Cooke et al., 2007, "Indigenous Well-being in Four Countries: An Application of the UNDP's Human Development Index to Indigenous Peoples in Australia, Canada, New Zealand, and the United States.," *BMC International Health and Human Rights* 7: 9.

42. United Nations, 2007, *United Nations Declaration on the Rights of Indigenous Peoples* <www.un.org/esa/socdev/unpfii/documents/ DRIPS_en.pdf>.

43. Royal Commission on Aboriginal Peoples (RCAP), 1996, *Report of the Royal Commission on Aboriginal Peoples,* Indian and Northern Affairs; Truth and Reconciliation Commission of Canada (TRC), 2015, *TRC Final Report* <http://www.trc.ca/websites/trcinstitution/index. php?p=3>.

44. J. Smylie and M. Firestone, 2016, "The Health of Indigenous

People," in D. Raphael (ed.), *Social Determinants of Health: Canadian Perspectives,* third edition, Canadian Scholars' Press.

45. G. Picot, 2004, *The Deteriorating Economic Welfare of Immigrants and Possible Causes,* Statistics Canada.

46. Organisation for Economic Cooperation and Development(OECD), 2016, *Gender Wage Gap* <oecd.org/gender/data/genderwagegap.htm>; United Nations Human Development Program (UNDP), 2015, *Human Development Report* <hdrstats.undp.org/en/indicators/126.html>.

47. A. Pederson, D. Raphael and E. Johnson, 2010, "Gender, Race, and Health Inequalities," in T. Bryant, D. Raphael, and M. Rioux (eds.), *Staying Alive: Critical Perspectives on Health, Illness, and Health Care,* second edition, Canadian Scholars' Press.

48. M. Haworth-Brockman, 2015, "Women and Health in Manitoba," in L. Fernandez, S. MacKinnon and J. Silver (eds.), *The Social Determinants of Health in Manitoba,* second edition, CCPA-Manitoba.

49. Council of Canadians with Disabilities, 2009, *From Vision to Action: Building an Inclusive and Accessible Canada: A National Action Plan,* Council of Canadians with Disabilities <ccdonline.ca/en/socialpolicy/actionplan/inclusive-accessible-canada>.

50. Organisation for Economic Co-operation and Development (OECD), 2015, *Society at a Glance, 2015 Indicators.*

51. Organisation for Economic Co-operation and Development (OECD), 2016, *Health Expenditure and Financing* <stats.oecd.org/index.aspx?DataSetCode=HEALTH_STAT>.

52. D. Raphael and A. Curry-Stevens, 2016, "Surmounting the Barriers: Making Action on the Social Determinants of Health a Public Policy Priority," in D. Raphael (ed.), *Social Determinants of Health: Canadian Perspectives,* third edition, Canadian Scholars' Press.

Chapter 7: What Needs to Be Done?

1. D. Langille, 2016, "Follow the Money: How Business and Politics Shape our Health," in D. Raphael (ed.), *Social Determinants of Health: Canadian Perspectives,* third edition, Canadian Scholars' Press.

2. Conference Board of Canada, 2016, *How Canada Performs: A Report Card on Canada* <www.conferenceboard.ca/hcp/default.aspx>.

3. See *Practising Public Scholarship: Experiences and Possibilities Beyond the Academy* for an exploration of the responsibility of academics to their communities <wiley.com/WileyCDA/WileyTitle/ productCd-1405189126.html>.

4. D. Langille, 2016, "Follow the Money."

5. Canadian Population Health Initiative (CPHI), 2004, *Select Highlights on Public Views of the Determinants of Health*; K. Shankardass et al., 2012, "Public Awareness of Income-Related Health Inequalities in Ontario, Canada," *International Journal for Equity in Health* 11 (26); Lofters et al., 2014, "How Do People Attribute Income-Related Inequalities in Health? A Cross-Sectional Study in Ontario, Canada," *PloS One,* 9 (1): e85286.

6. J. Mikkonen and D. Raphael, 2010, *Social Determinants of Health: The Canadian Facts* <http://www.thecanadianfacts.org/>.

7. Public Health Agency of Canada, 2010, *The 2010 Report on the Integrated Pan-Canadian Healthy Living Strategy* <phac-aspc.gc.ca/ hp-ps/hl-mvs/ipchls-spimmvs-eng.php>.

8. Sudbury and District Health Unit, 2011, *Let's Start a Conversation About Health … and Not Talk About Health Care at All* <youtube. com/watch?v=QboVEEJPNX0>.

9. See CBC, 2014, "Saturated Fat Alone Doesn't Predict Heart Disease Risk" <cbc.ca/news/health/saturated-fat-alone-doesn-t-predict-heart-disease-risk-1.2576252> and CBC, 2016, "Cholesterol in Diet Advice Overturned in U.S." <cbc.ca/news/health/ cholesterol-food-1.3394391>.

10. D. Raphael, May 11, 2014, "Why Are Canadians Not Being Told the Truth about Disease?" *Hamilton Spectator* <hthespec.com/

opinion-story/4405922-why-are-canadians-not-being-told-the-truth-about-disease-/>; D. Raphael, July 4, 2014, "Dealing with Symptoms, Not Disease: Corporate Influence in Nonprofit Organizations Neglects the Health Effects of Poverty," *Hamilton Spectator* <thespec.com/opinion-story/4612455-dealing-with-symptoms-not-disease/>.

11. M. Bartley, 1995, "Medicine and the Media: Deprived of Health," *British Medical Journal* 310 (6978): 539; M.J. Commers, G. Visser, and E. De Leeuw, 2000, "Representations of Preconditions for and Determinants of Health in the Dutch Press," *Health Promotion International* 15 (4): 321–332; B. Westwood and G. Westwood, 1998, "Assessment of Newspaper Reporting of Public Health and the Medical Model: A Methodological Case Study," *Health Promotion International* 14 (1): 53–64; M. Hayes et al., 2007, "Telling Stories: News Media, Health Literacy and Public Policy in Canada," *Social Science and Medicine* 54: 445–457.

12. M. Gasher et al., 2007, "Spreading the News: Social Determinants of Health Reportage in Canadian Daily Newspapers," *Canadian Journal of Communication* 32 (3): 557–574.

13. D. Raphael, 2011, "Mainstream Media and the Social Determinants of Health in Canada: Is It Time to Call It a Day?" *Health Promotion International* 26 (2): 220–229.

14. To join the list, go to <https://listserv.yorku.ca/archives/sdoh.html>.

15. K. Banting and J. Myles (eds.), 2013, *Inequality and the Fading of Redistributive Politics*, UBC Press.

16. G. Esping-Andersen, 1990, *The Three Worlds of Welfare Capitalism*, Princeton University Press.

17. D. Brady, 2009, *Rich Democracies, Poor People: How Politics Explain Poverty*, Oxford University Press.

18. See more about the Perth and Huron project at <https://www.policyalternatives.ca/publications/reports/calculating-living-wage-perth-and-huron-counties#sthash.IYkm7uyc.dpuf>.

19. E. Broadbent, February 21, 2009, "Barbarism Lite: The Political Attack on Social Rights," *Toronto Star* <www.thestar.com/comment/article/590845>.

APPENDIX

KEY RESOURCES ON THE SOCIAL DETERMINANTS OF HEALTH IN CANADA

Books

Bryant, Toba. 2016. *Health Policy in Canada,* second edition. Toronto: Canadian Scholars Press.

Raphael, Dennis. 2011. *Poverty in Canada: Implications for Health and Quality of Life,* second edition. Toronto: Canadian Scholars' Press.

____ (ed.). 2012. *Tackling Inequalities in Health: Lessons from International Experiences.* Toronto: Canadian Scholars' Press.

____ (ed.). 2016. *Social Determinants of Health: Canadian Perspectives,* third edition. Toronto: Canadian Scholars' Press.

Smith, Katherine, Clare Bambra, and Sarah Hill (eds.). 2016. *Health Inequalities: Critical Perspectives.* Oxford, UK: Oxford University Press.

Policy and Advocacy Organizations Addressing the Social Determinants of Health

Broadbent Institute <http://www.broadbentinstitute.ca>

Caledon Institute of Social Policy <www.caledoninst.org>

Campaign 2000 <www.campaign2000.ca>

Canada without Poverty <www.cwp-csp.ca/Blog>

Canadian Centre for Policy Alternatives <www.policyalternatives.ca>

Canadian Labour Congress <http://canadianlabour.ca>

Canadians for Tax Fairness <http://www.taxfairness.ca>

Child Care Advocacy Association of Canada <http://ccaac.ca>

Childcare Resource and Research Unit <www.childcarecanada.org>

Cooperative Housing Federation <www.chfcanada.coop/index.asp>

Disabled Women's Network <http://www.dawncanada.net>

Food Banks Canada <http://foodbankscanada.ca>

Food Secure Canada <http://foodsecurecanada.org>

Health Providers Against Poverty <http://healthprovidersagainstpoverty.
ca>

Institute for Work & Health <www.iwh.on.ca>

National Aboriginal Health Organization <www.naho.ca>

ODSP Action Coalition <www.odspaction.ca>

Ontario Women's Health Network <www.owhn.on.ca>

Upstream <http://www.thinkupstream.net>

Wellesley Institute <http://wellesleyinstitute.com>

Media Resources

How Canada Stacks up again other Nations <http://vimeo.
com/33346501>

*Let's Start a Conversation About Health ... and Not Talk About Health Care
at All* <www.youtube.com/watch?v=QboVEEJPNX0>

The Political Economy of Health Inequalities <http://www.youtube.com/
watch?v=-NCTYqAub8g>

Poor No More (2010) <www.poornomore.ca>

Population Health: The New Agenda (2009) Vancouver Coastal Health
Unit <https://vimeo.com/12167810>

Social Inequalities in Health <http://www.santemontreal.qc.ca/iss/en/>

Unnatural Causes: Is Inequality Making us Sick? (2008) California
Newsreel <www.unnaturalcauses.org.>

Website Resources

Canadian Public Health Association Policy Statements <http://www.
cpha.ca/en/programs/policy.aspx>

EU Social Determinants and Health Inequalities <http://tinyurl.com/

hxdf2v7>

National Collaborating Centre for Aboriginal Health <http://www.
nccah-ccnsa.ca/en/>

National Collaborating Centre for Determinants of Health <http://www.
nccdh.ca/>

National Collaborating Centre for Healthy Public Policy <http://www.
ncchpp.ca/en/>

Public Health Agency of Canada <www.phac-aspc.gc.ca/ph-sp/
approachapproche/index-eng.php>

Social Determinants of Health: The Canadian Facts <www.
thecanadianfacts.org>

WHO Social Determinants of Health <www.who.int/
social_determinants/en/>

INDEX